OTHER BOOKS BY GARY PAULSEN
PUBLISHED BY HARCOURT BRACE & COMPANY

Eastern Sun, Winter Moon

The Madonna Stories

Winterdance

FOR CHILDREN

Harris and Me

Sisters/Hermanas

Clabbered Dirt,
Sweet Grass

Clabbered Dirt, Sweet Grass

GARY PAULSEN

Paintings by
Ruth Wright Paulsen

A HARVEST BOOK
HARCOURT BRACE & COMPANY
San Diego   New York   London

Requests for permission to make copies
of any part of the work should be mailed to:
Permissions Department
Harcourt Brace & Company
6277 Sea Harbor Drive
Orlando, Florida 32887-6777

Library of Congress Cataloging-in-Publication Data
Paulsen, Gary.
Clabbered dirt, sweet grass / by Gary Paulsen;
illustrated by Ruth Wright Paulsen.—1st ed.
p.   cm.
ISBN 0-15-118101-2
ISBN 0-15-600052-0 (pbk.)
I. Title.
PS 3566.A834C53   1992
813'.54—dc20   92-3485

Designed by Michael Farmer
Printed in the United States of America
First Harvest edition 1994
A B C D E

Foreword

SOMETIMES BOOKS SEEM TO HAPPEN IN STRANGE WAYS, COME from strange places.

This book happened sitting on the back of a dead horse in the woods of northern Minnesota with soft snow falling and ice and dogs and winter all around, in the quiet sigh of an old man's life.

We did not have a phone, but a neighbor came to our house one day and said that he'd received a call about a dead horse and told the man to bring it.

We were training dogs for the Iditarod and it was common for people to bring us large animals that had died or had to be put down. Horses, cattle, pigs—we used them for dog food. Since it was winter it was possible to keep them and use them all season. It made good food, excellent food, and kept the animals from going to waste, so when the call came about the horse I just assumed it was a horse that had died of age or of pneumonia (which happened fairly often in early winter), nodded and told the neighbor we would be ready.

But not ready. Not for what came.

Two hours passed and a logging truck pulled into the drive. It was the size of truck that could carry sixteen full cords of wood, an open-bed semi with a large hydraulic arm ending in a clamshell grasper for lifting logs. Our driveway was narrow and threaded through trees so I couldn't see the trailer of the truck until the driver had jacked it around and backed into our yard and up next to the kennel.

There was a dead horse on the back, lying on its side. It was a light brown, almost a tan, and easily the largest horse I had ever seen. Even dead on its side it stood higher than some ponies and seemed to fill the whole semi bed of the truck. It was lying with its feet toward me and the bottoms looked larger than frying pans, great round flats of hooves.

As I stood, staring, the left door opened on the truck. The driver climbed out and over to the back of the truck without touching the ground and settled into the seat that controlled the hydraulic arm, worked the levers, and poised the lifters over the horse.

"Where do you want it?"

I motioned next to the truck, near the kennel. We had forty some dogs then and they were going insane, smelling the horse, knowing that it was for them. The driver nodded, looked over the side and deftly, almost surgically, set the clamshells around the middle of the horse and lifted it. The truck leaned when the weight went off center and I thought it would tip because he had not put down the brace arms, but he lowered the horse quickly to the ground and let the truck settle back in.

All this time the door on the passenger side of the truck had remained closed. I had seen somebody inside but could tell nothing of him due to the angle and height of the cab.

The door now opened and an old man stepped down from the truck.

To a point age is of course relative and it is hard to tell by appearances. Some are old, done, ended at forty and look it and some are never done. Norman Vaughn ran the Iditarod when he was eighty-three and I was hard pressed at almost exactly half his age to keep up with him.

But this man had gone past the relative point in aging. He was old enough so that his hands were bent with it, crooked with it and his back curved over where it would not be straight again and his cap sat low on his head. He wore a denim coat-jacket, the long kind, and it seemed to hide his whole body as he lowered to the ground and turned to me.

He was wearing a billed wool cap with the ear flaps down and the bill momentarily hid his eyes until he looked up and I could see they were bright blue, snow on sky blue beneath shaggy old-hair eyebrows.

"Gunnar," he said, holding out his hand. "Gunnar Pederson . . ." He started to say more as we shook hands but stopped because the trucker had moved back into the cab of the truck and revved the diesel so the noise took over everything, even the dogs, and he began driving out of the driveway, leaving the old man standing with me.

"He must get a load of wood from near here, north," Gunnar said. "He'll come back for me later . . ."

I nodded. It seemed strange that he would stay and the other leave, but I thought perhaps he did not like to drive or sit and wait in the truck.

"It is my horse," he said. "We had time together and now he is gone."

The truck was gone and the dogs were quieting, small whines, begs as they looked at the horse, and in the quiet his voice seemed to be more than it was, more than an old man saying something. It rang. *It is my horse. We had time together and now he is gone.*

"I thought," he said, "I would tell you about this horse."

He turned away and spit and went to the horse, lying on its side in the snow, and sat on the horse's front shoulder and motioned for me to come and sit next to him.

I had not moved all this time, had been thinking that I would go and get a cup of coffee for him, but when he beckoned I went to him and sat on the horse next to him and looked at the ground.

Surprisingly the horse was still very warm, soft, felt alive though the temperature was well below freezing and it had been dead for I thought some time.

"This horse had the name of Harold," he said, "because I had many years ago a son named Harold until they took him, the army took him and didn't give him back and his hair was this color of the horse. Is that something, to name a horse the same as a son?"

I said nothing. Something in me, some small place left from before I had moved into the woods, some small city place made a little wonder about how it was strange to be sitting in the evening light with gentle snow falling, sitting on a dead horse named Harold. Then it was gone, the thought, just as that other life was gone and would always be gone.

"Harold came as new as anything I ever got," he said. "Harold the horse and Harold the son. I had a mare name of Marcy came from a neighbor couldn't pull, the mare, and I had her bred and along came Harold and I watched him born and knew he would be a good horse. Harold."

He put his hand down on the horse's neck next to his leg, where the shoulder turned to neck and he petted the horse. His hands were bare and I saw snow fall on them and it didn't melt fast but seemed to hang there, caught on the old hands. He petted the horse, then took a pair of leather chopper mittens out of his pocket and put them on.

He was crying.

I hadn't seen it at first, but when he moved his head as he

put the mittens on I saw the edges of his eyes and they were tearing and he brushed them with his sleeve, the inside of the sleeve, almost a feminine gesture, the way he turned his arm over to brush, and I thought, God I am seeing more of him than I am supposed to see and I turned away. There are parts to see and parts not to see, not to know, not to write about.

"Look," I said. "It isn't necessary for me to have this horse for the dogs. I can borrow the neighbor's tractor and pull him back into the woods and when spring comes and the ground softens we can bury him . . ."

"No."

Again, a strong voice. A ring. *No.*

"Harold started new, was new and now has to end, but if he is in the dogs, part of the dogs, he will go on and it is the way things work, that way."

I said nothing. I did not understand just yet what he meant but running dogs for me had become more than just running dogs, had become mystical, a kind of prayer every time I ran them, and I was ready to try and know what he meant. The snow seemed light, seemed to float, and where it had been dirty, where the dogs had eaten meat and left blood, it was beginning to look clean and white.

"He was not the first horse I ever had," he said, "Harold. Not even the third or fourth. We used to do all things with horses, all things. Until they came out with the tractors that's all we had, horses, and at one time my father and his father

xii

working the farm I have now had six horses, six horses that shook the ground when they walked. Sometimes in the winter we used them to haul pulp wood from the woods into the railroad sidings to be picked up by the paper companies and there were so many horses it was hard to count them." He stopped, took a breath. "Like dogs. Like your dogs are to you, that's how horses were to us. Just the same."

Ahh, I thought—the prayer. They were that way, like the prayer of running dogs. "I see," I said, and I thought I did.

He nodded. "All you have to do is close your eyes and you can see. You *can* see. All of it, the way it was then when we used horses. Listen, now, listen to this about how it was to plow with them, two and four horse teams pulling the plows in the hot early summer mornings when we broke new ground. They had to stop at the end of each row to blow and cool down and we had boys to come out in the fields with buckets to pour cool water on them and then we would by God do another row. And another. The goddamn soil turned like black butter, so rich if you threw a seed in it it would grow while you watched. And that was before all the chemicals, all before that. Jesus Christ, you should have seen it then, seen how the soil turned. It breaks now, breaks and crumbles like dry shit, but it used to come off the mullboard like thick black cream, over and over and over."

He stopped and I thought would not talk anymore but it was only to catch his breath.

"Listen. Listen now," he said, and leaned to spit away from the body of the horse, spit a dark tobacco hole in the new snow. "Listen, listen now and I will tell you . . ."

And he did.

He told me all of his life and of Harold and the other horses and his dead son and his wife and dairy cows that he had and a daughter gone to a city and no goddamn good because she wasn't married yet and of how his wife who was dead could cook like five other wives when she lived and his farm, oh God, his farm.

His farm.

That had belonged to his father and his father's father, the farm, torn from the woods with horses jerking the stumps when the first Pederson came from the old country.

His farm.

Soil handed down from one father to the next son to be a father and the next son to be a father, handed down with the horses and the soil and the smells and the sounds, all handed down, and he told me of it all.

Every part of it.

Sitting there on the dead horse in the quiet snow coming down on us and the side of the horse, clean white snow, he told me all of everything he was and had been and would be, told me of the farm and the life he had, and when he was done—still crying softly—and I could see that he was really done in the light from the house across the kennel and not just taking another breath, when he was truly done he turned to me and said:

"And so the dogs must have him, must eat of him and make him not to end so that he can go on, Harold, and on and on because the farm, the farm will not. My son will not farm nor his sons and the brush will take it back, the farm, all of it . . ."

Then he stopped, stood and walked toward the dogs, stopped and petted each of them when they jumped on him, went to each one and took his mittens off and touched them the same way he had touched the horse while talking and when he was done he walked away, out the driveway to where he would meet the logging truck. I sat on the horse for all this time, thinking of the things he had said, rubbed my fingers in the hair near the back of the horse and watched him walking into the darkness and thought:

Who will eat the man?

How can it end that way? The horse goes on but not the man, not the farm—how can that be? Who will make him go on and on so that the things of him, the way of him will not stop, will not end?

SPRING

CALVES COME EARLY IN THE SPRING.

It was how we knew winter would die, would end.

In the dark of the barn night when it was still cold enough outside to make things break, in the warm dark night of the closed barn they came, and when we would open the door in the morning to start chores we could smell them, the new calves.

It was more than rich, the smell—more even than an odor. An air, a new air would be in the barn, coming out, a new air of life.

Afterbirth stink mixed all hot and wet with new milk, thick milk that came so full that it ran from the cow whether the calf was nursing or not, ran on the ground in streams and they would take the calves, the grown-ups, take the calves and put them in pens at the end of the barn. A day old, not even a

3

full day, and they stood in the pen and wobbled and fell and wobbled and fell while we climbed in with them, the children, and rolled in the new straw with them and petted them and hugged them because they were closer to us, the calves, than the adults were and meant that the back of winter was broken and spring was starting.

They did not know how to drink from buckets when they first came. The calves were not allowed to nurse because it would ruin the cow for milking and besides, there was too much milk in each cow for any one calf, any five calves. So when the cows were milked a small amount was poured into a bucket and the children had to teach them to drink. They would suck on anything, the end of our coats, mittens, ears, and we would stick our fingers in their mouths and start them sucking and lower our hands into the warm milk in the bucket so they would suck the milk up through our fingers. It took them only a short time to learn to suck the milk directly, slamming their heads into the bucket as they would slam them into the cow to make the milk flow so that milk splashed up and out and into our faces, down our clothes, hot new milk, spring milk.

Later there would be baby pigs in the hog shed on the side of the barn, rows of pigs to look like little pink toys digging for nipples and making the small sounds that all new animals make and still later, when spring was close to turning into summer, there would be lambs. New lambs to spring and jump

4

and they all have a part in it, the way farms were then, but were not as much of spring as the calves.

And milking.

Milking was all the time, not just in spring, but it was different then because the milk smelled, the air was of calves. It was regular, so fitted into our rituals that it became more than just chores.

Chores.

"It's time to do chores."

Really always meant it was time to milk. Up at four in the morning to sit in the kitchen, the end of winter dark, while the grown-ups drank cup after cup of black coffee and leaned nearer the wood stove to soak the heat to get them across the dark cold to the barn. We watched them and listened to the fire and the coughing of the old ones as they rose and came downstairs to do chores.

Four to seven in the morning, then a full day of work, then five to eight at night. The chores. Milking. And it became more than work, became something of spirit or grace, almost a benediction.

Out to the barn to feed hay and silage and clean the gutters and start milking. Not with machines.

By hand.

Much is made of bonds between man and animals, horses, dogs. But this is beyond that. The milk stool is set just so and the forehead is put into the soft warm spot where the cow's gut meets her back leg so that the stomach rumbles and gurgles as part of the person's thinking, breathing, low sounds and the hands work in a rhythm perhaps as old as all rhythms, the movement that is the giving of milk, so that the person becomes the calf and the cow the mother and the milk hisses and sputters into the bucket, into the white foam, unless the barn cat sitting in the aisle begs by sitting up and waving its front paws like a small bear. Then the stream is aimed and squirted into the cat's mouth, a quick move from the rhythm and back while the cat gulps and jumps up to sit on the cow's back to clean itself, the same back where it sleeps in the winter nights to stay warm.

Chores.

All the milk is carried to the small room at the end of the barn where the hand crank separator is bolted to the floor and the young ones take turns cranking the flywheel faster and faster in the high whine to spin the milk and separate the cream.

Gold, an aunt called it—cream was gold and eggs were gold because the money from cream and eggs went to the house, went for cloth to sew into dresses or curtains or a new oilcloth with red flowers printed against green leaves for the kitchen table. Gold that poured out in a thick stream, cream into the tall cream bucket and milk into a regular bucket to be fed back to the calves or stored in milk cans to take into town to the creamery.

With milking done, chores done, it was time to eat breakfast before starting work. Food five times a day. Breakfast, forenoon lunch, dinner, afternoon lunch and supper. Each time a meal. Breakfast would almost always be strips of meat fried in butter and a huge pan of raw fried potatoes peeled the night before and left to soften all night. Or pancakes. Piles of pancakes with syrup made from a metal can of syrup concentrate that came in the shape of a log cabin and when it was empty and licked and relicked and rinsed we could cut holes in it and play that it was a house for little stick men and machinery.

By seven the chores were done and breakfast was done and it was time to go to work and all worked, young, old, all, and if we were too young to work we went with and "helped" those who did work.

The barn had to be cleaned, the manure taken out to the fields and spread, and this meant the horses, the work team.

Jim and Digger.

Always names that way. Jim. Bob. Digger. Mary. Always short names to be said in friendship and maybe sometimes gruffly.

Huge horses. Huge to adults, enormous mountains to young people, and we would go into the barns in the spring and sit on them in their stalls while they ate, listen to their chewing and feel the gentleness of them, climb their legs and hang on their manes and feed them oats out of our hand, the great heads lowering gently and the flubbery lips tickling our fingers as they took each and every small kernel.

Once a boy ran off, many times he ran off, and once he went into North Dakota running and decided to become a carnie so he went to a fairground the night before the carnival people came. He wanted to sleep, and lay in the stalls in the empty horse barn and fell asleep in the straw. He awakened in the morning and there were workhorse teams standing over him, a forest of thick legs and muscles, teams brought in during the night for the pulling competitions, and somebody had covered him with a feed sack to keep him warm and the horses had stood over him all night, carefully moving their feet around him to not hurt him, not touch him, not awaken him.

Harnessing was when the men became the horses and the horses became men. The harnesses smelled of sweat and neat's-foot oil and jingled with chains, and the men moved their hands over the horses in small caresses, putting the collar on and the hames and stretching the harness back over their backs, all while speaking the low soft tones that went from the men into the horses, small talking.

"Now Jim we're going to set in for some work today and I'll be working with you and ain't it a good day for it . . ." And then in a lower voice, gruff, commands. "Back, out and back . . ."

As the men work them backward out of the stalls to walk

8

them out of the big door in the end of the barn and hook them to the stone boat (sledge) for cleaning the barn.

"Back, back, around, back around, there, hold it hold it hold it . . ."

And they hook the trace chains to the singletrees on the stone boat and then back into the barn to stand while we forked and shoveled the manure in the gutters onto the stone boat and when it is full, rich and steaming, the horses snatched it out of the door and through the mud and spring slush to the fields, dragging the load easily, hardly breathing. We stood one on each side of the stone boat and threw the manure out with forks, spreading it as we threw in fans of steam and ammonia stink until we had emptied it and then slapping the reins on the horses' rumps.

"Up, Jim! Pick it up, Digger!"

Into a full impossible mammoth lumbering gallop, great hooves throwing up clods and mud and manure and slush in our faces, all over our fronts as we careened across the field, the stone boat flying from lump to lump and across the ditch and down the yard to end in a spray of muck by the barn.

Spring.

Hide in the haymow and talk. Climb up in the top of the peak of the barn roof and jump down in the soft hay, hang on the overhead rail or ride the trip rope down and fall, somersault and fall, dive and fall, scream and do Tarzan yells and

9

fall into the hay forever, into the winter-old timothy hay, to fall and fall and finally stop, looking up through a tunnel of soft warm clean hay and then lie and talk. Haymow talk. Haymow spring talk about what would be, what could be, what we hoped would be; spring haymow talk about stolen moments, stolen kisses and hidden candy and bright secrets that nobody outside the haymow could ever ever ever know about. Ever.

Spring.

And equipment to repair, to get ready for summer and work. Plowshares to be taken into the blacksmith in town, and the smithy is just across from the store where the shelves are full of all the things there are in the world. Hard candy that looks like ribbons with strips of color in glass jars on the counter and pocketknives and cans of peaches in syrup so sweet it sticks on hands for a week, all to eat and look at while the blacksmith is working on the plowshares and shoeing the horses to get them ready for summer work.

The plowshares come off the forge red and to the edge of white, trailing sparks, and take the hammer in dull rings to squeeze the steel back out into an edge, sharp and shiny and tight, and the horses stand, stand for their shoes while they are put hot on the hoof, held a moment in a blue swirl of smoke that stinks of burned hair and feathers, sticky sweet smoke that curls like oil in the air, before they are splashed in water to cool before nailing them on. They stand, the horses,

as they stand for all things unless they forget themselves and lean on the smithy while he's working on them only to move away gently, slowly, when he swears and hits their side with his elbow or the flat of his hand.

"Goddammit, Digger, you're on me like a house, get the *hell* over."

And a ton of horse, a mountain of horse, all the horse there is leans away from the small tight-corded hard little man in the leather apron and burned eyebrows whose son stands and works the crank on the bellows the way the young ones on the farm work the hand crank on the separator. The horse leans away and holds his foot up delicately while the smithy files around the nailed shoe to clean off jagged edges that could snag.

The plowshares shine like silver when they are pounded out, shine like sword silver, and the smithy runs his hands over them as if they were his, not ours, as if the horses were his, not ours, because he owned their shoes, their feet, as he owned the beauty of the plowshare, and so they were his too though he didn't use them or even see them used.

Spring.

There comes a spring day when school is impossible. Not difficult, nor boring, nor lengthy nor slow nor anything but just impossible. All winter in one room with the eighth grade on one side and the first grade on the other and all the other grades in the middle, and only one teacher except that the older children help the teacher with the younger ones, close around the stove in the winter writing with dusty white chalk on wood-rimmed slates we hold in our laps to make the letters, the perfect letters printed around the edges of the slates, the perfect A and the perfect B, biting tongues while we draw, the chalk scraping to make our teeth loose to make the perfect, perfect letters for the teacher to see and to nod and to smile. All impossible now. A world impossibly small in the warm opening explosion of spring until at last the teacher nods and the room stampedes into the cloak hall at the end for four-buckle overshoes with black gripper soles and then out into the warm new sun of the playground still in slush, mud, but cleansing, new. To sit and play marbles along the south side of the schoolhouse in the soft morning sun, playing for keeps, lusting after shooters and steelies and aggies and cat's-eyes, and running to play tag and pump-pump-pullaway-if-you-don't-come-I'll-pull-you-away or to see the teacher sitting on a piece of firewood by the wall and reading to the first and second graders, the breeze riffling the pages and their hair and her hair and the sun bright on the pages when she raises the book to show the pictures. See, see the fish and see the whales and see the red fire engines, and then lunch; sit to lunch next to the school with thick slices of hard crusted bread and honey with bits of comb in it and a pickle from last year's garden and a pint jar of rhubarb sauce sweet to the edge of sour and sour to the edge of sweet and on this day, this early day there can be no school. No studies because it is impossible, just impossible to think of anything school-like, and when the day is done and we head home in the wagons pulled by the teams it is a kind of victory and a kind of surrender at the same time. There will be more school and perhaps more winter but not on this day, not on this one grand hopeful brilliant impossible day.

Spring.

And it is time to open, clean, rip and gut the house. A whole winter of smells are there. Old clothes and drying mittens in back of the stove, manure on boots tracked in, and the hanging odor of the slop bucket by the door with potato peels and coffee grounds and lard scrapings for the pigs slathered into the indoor/outdoor smell of pine smoke from all the winter fires in the walls, the curtains, the floor, and air thick, thick with winter, so the first warm spring day all the windows and doors are opened and propped with sticks and air blows through. Even the attic where the young ones sleep in bare dormers without heat under mountains of quilts of colored patterns to look at in the mornings, in the morning light coming through frosty panes, bits of rag turned to beauty and the memory of Grandmother, no, Grandma sitting by the quilt frame in the small room next to the kitchen with the cold flat glare of winter coming through the window, working bits of brightness into the patterns, wearing small round glasses and a bun and a smile, a white false-teeth smile. Even the attic opened to the air and the clean fresh smell of spring winds, south winds to melt and make new, comes into all the rooms and lifts the curtains in little rippled kisses, washes them in air and carries winter finally, wonderfully and completely and utterly away.

Spring.

SUMMER

WORK, SUMMER WORK WAS NEVER FINISHED, NEVER TRULY begun, and could not be measured except with the honesty and gentleness of soul humor: remember when Alfred fell asleep with the fork halfway to his mouth during plowing that summer or when Knute stopped his team on the rake during haying and was sound asleep with his eyes wide open, and was it the third day or the fourth day without stopping shucking corn that Lydia just fell over, fell over and slept in the dust by the front door and her six months seven months eight months along . . .

Work.

Summer work.

From light to dark and then some, from up to drop, from beginning to . . . beginning again, never an end.

Plowing. Breaking the ground with a team of horses and a

one-bladed plow to sit upon; so hard, so many things to know and do that it seems something from another world, not just another time. Horses to know, to *know*, to feel, to smell, to understand, to train; horses to pull evenly so the plow and man will make a straight furrow in the early summer heat, sweat dripping down from the horses, sweat flies working around the fly shields, burrowing in the sweat to drink the blood, great ugly flies that twist and take meat with each bite; horses to watch, to learn from, to know so that with each furrow they do not collapse, do not stop but grow stronger and more true to the plow.

Tractors. Plowing not just with horses but with old tractors—F-12, F-20, Johnny-poppers, Minneapolis Moline—steel lugs on the back wheels, grinding, digging monsters that move only slightly faster than the horses; huge steel-levered suicide clutches to throw forward, still so new that old Agil says he can do better with horses and sometimes can, sometimes can until the heat comes up and the horses can't sweat enough to cool down and the tractor keeps going, keeps whining and popping and churning along, the big steel steering wheel with the steel knob that whips when the front wheels catch the furrow wrong and crack the bones in your knuckle and Uncle Hamish finding a way to put a wire on the knob tied to the clutch lever to hold the front wheel in the furrow just so, just so to keep the tractor going along and plowing while he dozes, sitting and dozing too long one day and plowing out the end of the field, across a small road and into the neighbor's field and across that field and into the neighbor's yard, plowing all the way, a straight line furrow while he slept, dragging broken fence and wire and brush in back of the plow.

Plowing. The first great music of summer. Plowing and watching the black dirt turn, the blue-black dirt so dark you can see into it turn and turn over and over like an earthen braid while the seagulls float over the blade of the plow in the hundreds, float on invisible air one foot, two feet above the turning black-beauty dirt, looking down for worms to grab and swallow without landing, to shoot up into the air while another gull swoops down for worms turning like gifts in the black rich earth.

Furrows straight. Straight aimed at a tree, then turn and straight aimed at a rock down the middle of the field, straight as a chalked line, straight as a machine, straight as cutting steel and a machine can make them straight, straight, *straight*.

"You can tell a man by how straight he plows," they say. "Crooked furrows mean loose thinking. Tell a man by how straight and how deep he plows. Too deep and he's wasting the rich part, wasting it deep and gone so's the roots can't reach it. Tell a man by how straight and deep he plows and how tall and neat his woodpile is and how sharp he keeps his axe and bucksaw and how clean his barn is and how his horse harness is loose and supple with oil and how his wheels don't squeak on his manure spreader and how even his corn grows and how plumb his granary wall is and how true his fences run and how fat and shiny his stock is and how short his stumps are when he cuts trees and how much he can lift— Oh, Jesus, yes, Karl Knutson could lift a calf and keep lifting it as it grew until he could lift a bull—or bend or hit or spit or swear or piss or laugh or eat or drink or scratch or fart or throw or fight or work, work, work, but mostly, mostly you can tell a man by how he plows."

Plowing. And when it is done and all the winter and spring and manure is turned under, nothing is finished at all, not finished so much as beginning.

Come in from plowing and drop the plow, shares worn for another year, shiny as silver plate, clean and polished to shine the sun back, drop the plow and back the old tractor to the disc, eat from a held plate while the tractor is being refueled, the green flywheel on the tractor pop-popping-pop-popping while the food is wolfed down, and then back, back to the same field to disc and break up the clean black furrows into a flat-black bed and when dark comes, ten o'clock dark, hard dark, back to the barn to help with chores to fall, fall into bed and up before light, up at two-thirty in the morning to smell, taste the air, and if there is no water in it, no rain, back to the field to finish discing, cutting it down, and then dragging it with a spiked-tooth harrow until it is broken, crumbled and rich like loamy black cake batter.

Uncles smile, laugh when they pick up the soil in their

hands and rub it against their pants, smile with faces burned
and dirted dark except for white circles around their eyes so
they seem always surprised, happy. Pick up the dirt and smile
and say:

"Drop a seed in this, drop a goddamn seed in this, and you
won't make the edge of the field before it's up to your knees,
tripping you . . ."

Pick up the soil and taste it, taste a piece of it and smell it
and throw it down and smile and say, "Clabbered dirt, sweet
grass," even though dirt doesn't clabber and sour, but still, still
there is a thing to taste there that tells things.

And yet only begun, the summer work.

Almost not started.

Each seed, each oat or barley or flax or wheat or corn seed
must be put into the earth. And covered. And tamped.

"Drilled," they say for seeding. "We have to drill tomorrow."

If it doesn't rain and if it isn't too heavy dew to work in the
early morning and if and if and if . . .

No rest again. Milking, chores until eleven, midnight, then
up at two-thirty to hook the horses to the old wooden-wheeled
seed drill. A bin with a wheel at each end and cutter discs and
tamping chains following along to drill the seeds in, the horses
moving evenly, gently up and back the field because the tractor
tears it up too much because the drill hasn't been changed
over to the tractor because, because "goddamn it I like to work
the horses and I hate the stink and noise of that goddamn

tractor," and each time the wheel turns it flips a gear cog and drops a seed, a measured seed down a flexible tube between the cutting discs into the ground, packed by the chain. Each time. Each seed. Eight feet wide, the drill, eight up and eight back dropping seeds to become wheat or oats or barley or flax.

And luck.

There is all luck in it, so much luck that they don't talk about it, the luck, don't say a word about it; so much luck they smile and shrug and pray to themselves while they work and wait for the bad things to come. If it doesn't rain the seeds won't come up; if it rains too much the seeds won't come up; if it rains but then doesn't rain again at the right time the seeds will come up but the plants will die; if the rain comes but comes too much the plants will die; if the rain doesn't come at first and the wind comes the topsoil will blow away enough to uncover the seeds and blow *them* away and they will die; if the rains come perfectly and the wind doesn't come but the mustard weeds get a good start the plants will be choked off; if everything works exactly right and the rains come at the right time but not too often and the wind doesn't come and the weeds don't overcome them the plants will grow and they will head and they will become ripe and grow golden and then, and then if the wind stays away and doesn't come to rip the heads loose and the hail doesn't come to flatten the stiff, brittle dying plants and grasshoppers don't come to eat what has grown, *then* there might be a harvest.

All luck.

And the luck doesn't stop there, what the luck means doesn't stop there. All the luck in the world has to come every year, in every part of every year, or there is not a harvest and then the luck, the bad luck will come and everything we are, all that we can ever be, all the Einsteins and babies and love and hate, all the joy and sadness and sex and wanting and liking and disliking, all the soft summer breezes on cheeks and first snowflakes, all the Van Goghs and Rembrandts and Mozarts and Mahlers and Thomas Jeffersons and Lincolns and Ghandis and Jesus Christs, all the Cleopatras and lovemaking and riches and achievements and progress, all of that, every single damn thing that we are or ever will be is dependent on six inches of topsoil and the fact that the rain comes when it's needed and does not come when it is not needed; everything, every . . . single . . . *thing* comes with that luck.

So much of it is luck that on a morning, a wet morning in June after chores, after the work of chores and the rain had made it too wet to work in the fields, rain that had come and kept coming for over a week, after such a rain in the soft gray light of a wet morning a boy saw an uncle leaning against the side of the old log barn, leaning there throwing up, looking at the water pouring off the barn roof, throwing up and crying softly to himself, and when the boy walked up to him he looked at the boy and the rain and said:

"Sometimes it's all just shit, isn't it?"

So terribly much of it is luck that even when the weather is perfect, dry and the fields waiting to work, even if all things are exactly right for working, when a Sunday comes around except for chores work stops and the luck, the fates, God is honored. After milking everybody takes turns at the sink pump and washes from the waist up, digging in the ears, pouring cold water over heads, whistling and squealing when the water hits, and into new overalls, brittle clean shirts and dresses, and into the back of the old truck, the old 1937 Ford with cable brakes for the ride three miles to church.

Church. Everybody sitting in rows, the children next to the parents down in a row while the minister talks not of luck nor of crops but bellows against sin, tears at religious weakness or lapses in faith like a spiritual pit bull, stamping the floor in back of the pulpit, holding his finger like a gun aimed at members of the congregation until even the young ones who are bored beyond thought, beyond living, even the young ones who think the service must go on and on until they are old and dead, even they must sit up and hear the thundering word of God, and when it is at last done and the hymns have been hummed and roared and the benediction laid like salve on injured eardrums and souls, finally then there is some peace.

Outside the church after shaking hands with the minister— "his hands are so soft, Carl, so soft and clean and unbroken and different, so soft like the hands of God must be, Carl, so soft because he is a good minister and studies all the time and

24

hasn't time to work"—outside there is a small time for talking. A very small time for visiting. Stand in groups by the trucks, men and women together, not touching but so close to touching it doesn't matter, stand and talk of . . . of . . . work, what else.

"Rocks—that east forty is all rocks. Pushed up by spring freezing and thawing. Damn rocks. Like riding a bucking bronco to plow in there but if I don't take it, take that forty, I don't have enough feed."

"Over to the south, that south twelve where the low spot is, the water is still standing there from the last rain and I can't get in there with the team. I'm going to lose that, four, four-and-a-half acres lost this summer."

"I've never seen anything like it, Mary—Mama is working on a quilt that is all in solid colors, star shapes, and so pretty it just takes your breath away to see it. Last year she crocheted a tablecloth and I'm afraid to use it, it's so pretty. She works and works all the time and she's over eighty. Yesterday I caught her in the barn with a fork, cleaning the calf pen. . . ."

A small time to talk, just a small time by the church in the Sunday noon sun while the minister stands by the door and smiles and shakes everybody's hand in front of the white, white church, and then the ride home in back of the truck, the breeze ruffling hair and clean shirts and dresses.

Home to change back into work clothes and a cold lunch, pork sandwiches on the same thick slabs of bread, vinegar potato salad with bits of salt and dusty mail-order pepper fresh on top, and milk brought up from the springhouse still tasting of the metal of the separator; home to a full stomach and to sit on the cool side of the house, the adults leaning back in chairs against the wall while the young ones sit on the ground, and no talk, not even small talk, no talk and no sound except for the birds, thousands of summer birds, and the dog barking at something down by the springhouse and a barn cat meowing as it weaves through legs begging for sandwich scraps, all for one incredible, free, glorious hour while the food settles. A stolen hour, the hour after church, after Sunday lunch, sitting in the shade on the cool side of the house. One clear, clean stolen hour—a gift from God, that hour. A pure and private gift from God.

Then work.

Summer work.

The rest of Sunday afternoon working on machinery and there is a kind of blessing to that, a Sunday blessing. Harness to be oiled and greased and rivets checked and trace chains replaced if they've snatched broken; wheels to be greased, oil to be changed, hooves to be rasped and evened, and the pump at the windmill, always broken in some way, the pump has to be repaired, working in the soft Sunday afternoon; everything broken during the week, worn and broken and tired including the human bodies, all that to be made new on the quiet Sunday afternoon while the children play in the sand by the pump-house, making small roads and fields for toy tractors and teams, and Uncle Olaf-Carl-Gustaf-Willard-Henry sits by the granary sharpening a sickle blade with a triangular-shaped hand stone and spits tobacco juice while he sings songs with parts missing that he learned in France where he fought the "Chermans" before, before, before . . .

There are not separations in the work, not spaces where one kind of work ends and another begins, but there are lines, blurred thin lines when a thing is finished and another thing is to start.

When the fields are worked to cream and everything is planted and the corn is "knee-high-by-the-Fourth-of-July" and cultivated to be in clean-green rows, cultivated by the team pulling a man sitting on the corn cultivator and the horses not stepping on a single corn plant because they know, they know what can be and what cannot be, when the corn is so clean the weeds seem never to have existed and the oats are green to the edge of purple and as flat on top as if a ruler had been drawn across them, when all that is done there is a line, a fine line, and it is time for hay.

Hay is the first time in the year when people come together to work, when one family is not enough and maybe two is not enough and so straws are drawn to see who goes first and everybody brings their horses and equipment to the first farm for haying.

Before baling, before tractors, the hay was cut with John

Deere mowers pulled by teams, the turning wheels making the mower cut with magic, magic mechanics. The wheels were cogged to the Pittman arm that worked the sickle bar and dropped the hay back over the bar with neat snick-snicks, dropped back like soldiers in the new smell of hay, clean hay mixed with the odor of hot oil on the sickle bar as it worked back and forth through the guards, clean hay and hot oil and every round the bar must be reoiled. Grass hay and timothy hay and alfalfa hay all dropped neatly back to lie, two, three mowers following each other until it was midmorning and time to stop for forenoon lunch and rest the teams.

The horses are pulled into the shade and covered with fly curtains to help with the horseflies, coming now in clouds as the summer heat brings the hatches out, and men feed the horses grain with feed bags on their noses and go to sit under trees away from the horses.

Red faces with a white line on the men's foreheads when their caps come off and a red V edged with white on their neck when their shirt is opened and bib overalls with turnip pocket watches and a fob of metal made in the shape of a team of horses and backs curved with strength and load and tiredness, the men come and sit beneath the trees and eat sandwiches and cake and drink black coffee from quart jars wrapped in feed sacks to keep the coffee warm.

"Hot coffee for hot weather," somebody says, somebody

always says, somebody always has to say, and somebody else says:

"Yes, and hot coffee for cold weather, too."

And they smile and laugh politely and eat without speaking, eat with cheek muscles working like cables, eat with hunger so great it makes the jaws ache, eat and drink coffee until the grounds come and then chew the grounds and eat one more piece of cake while the horses rest, all without speaking.

Until forenoon lunch is done. Then they lean back against trees or rocks, in the shade, always in the shade, and roll cigarettes from Bull Durham sacks kept in their bibs, roll them neatly without wasting two crumbs of the small foul tobacco, roll them and light them with wooden matches that smell in the air for hours after they are struck, and lean back and talk of the work.

The work.

"Damn sickle bar caught a grouse sitting to nest and took her head off. I saved the eggs in the tool box to put under a banty hen."

Every year, every haying it happens that a grouse or two or five doesn't get off the nest and is killed by the sickle bar and eggs are placed beneath banty hens; small mean vicious child-chasing wonderful banties, which are too small to eat and whose eggs are too tiny to use but everybody has because they are so wonderfully prolific, are always sitting on eggs to hatch and will hatch and mother anybody's eggs, even grouse, and so every summer and early fall the farmyard is filled with grouse chicks, exploding, flying from tree to tree until they understand they are wild and not limited to the farm and can leave, do leave, and are gone then, to return perhaps in winter when feed is scarce in the woods and they remember how much grain there was on the farm. But not just grouse chicks. All things. A box in back of the kitchen stove can have baby ducks from a mallard killed by a skunk, or small birds or baby squirrels or rabbits pulled in by the children, always something small and cute and alive from the woods to nurture, raise, send back. Once a beautiful otter that lived in the stock tank all summer and ate bits of meat from fingers and again a beautiful lynx kit taken from a mother killed by a train, found near the tracks and the mother's torn body, and raised to adulthood; a great tufted lynx that came to beg in the barn for milk and sat on the cows in the winter to stay warm, found in the summer, found in the haying time when it was still new.

Luck must come again. When the hay is cut and laying-to-dry it must not rain, cannot rain until it is stacked or it may be ruined and now, now they watch the sky more than ever, the men sitting on the mowers. Watch the blue, watch for mare's tails, hair clouds, painted brushes of hair clouds that will come before a front, come before the thick clouds of rain, come slithering over the horizon, the mare's tails. The mowers move, one after another, move and snick-snick the grass down

in the smell of hot oil and the men watch the sky and the women watch the sky and finally even the children watch the sky, knowing that if they watch, all watch, the clouds will not come.

And when they do not, when the luck holds and the rain doesn't come and all the hay is cut and dried for a full warm day in the sun, the raking starts.

Sulkies, the rakes. Two large steel wheels twelve feet apart with a set of curved spring-tines between them and a seat to sit on and a foot lever to trip the rake and raise the tines when they are full of the new hay. There is no weight to them and the teams know this, feel this, and the rake becomes a toy to them, something to play with; faster and faster they rake, the wheels flying, the rake dumping load next to load to form rows and then turn, turn and come down the row to make piles for picking up later, and all of it faster and faster until it is necessary to lean back on the reins to hold the team while tripping the rake and steering the team and always, always being careful of the foot pedal. Stories about the foot pedal on trip rakes fill the forenoon lunches, the dinners, the times when the horses are resting from the heat and flies. Everybody knows of somebody, sometimes many people, who have gotten their foot caught in the trip pedal and the team ran away and the man was dragged to death in back of the rake; it is never anybody to see, to know personally, but always somebody in the next town, the next county. He had a white horse in his team and white horses are bad luck you know, always bad luck, because bees come to them and a swarm of bees landed on the rump of the white horse and the team went crazy and ran away and the man's foot caught in the trip pedal and he couldn't get free, couldn't jump away, and was dragged to death they say, sitting smoking Bull Durham cigarettes with scarred and dirty hands that eat a sandwich or a cookie down to the part their fingers hold and then throw that away, never eat the part you touch. Yup, he had a white horse and the goddamn bees swarmed on her and that was it, or his team was shy and a piece of sacking blew across the field and they panicked and ran away and his foot got caught in the trip pedal or a Model T went by on the road and backfired and they ran away and his foot got caught in the trip pedal . . .

Hay stories. They always led to other stories. Stories of great tragedy, horrible loss. Yes it's bad about the horses running away but cousin Bets had a two-year-old boy name of Sonny who somehow someway someday got into the pigpen and she didn't know it until she was walking past the pigpen and saw her brood sow eating on one of his arms— couldn't find anything else to bury until they shot the sow and cut her open. Christ. Smoke and look at the ground, silent, then, simply: Christ. Pigs are always good for hay stories, and corn choppers, silage choppers, cows with new calves, stallions and bulls or bad dogs. Always a child. Always a child wanders into a pen or falls into a piece of machinery and nobody misses him/her until later and the small body is found or sometimes not found, never found, and in back of each farm small graves from before, always before. Small graves from the first ones, the homesteaders who would sometimes have one child live in four, five; they'd make two, three years old and then die, and there are the small graves, sometimes with tiny stones if they could afford it and a little lamb on top, small graves from the hay stories.

With the hay in piles it was time for the sweep rakes; a large wooden-tined basket between two horses to go down the row of piles to gather them and carry them, three, four piles at a time to the stacker.

Haystacks and stackers were made for children. The stacker like a dinosaur sitting in the field, a large wooden-tined bucket like the sweep rakes on one end and ropes leading through pulleys to a team of stacker horses to pull the bucket up and up and over the top to dump the hay higher and higher to make the stacks that didn't look like hay, looked like round loaves of bread in the fields. The stacker horses did nothing all day but move forward to pull the rope to dump the stacker, then back, back to get ready for the next load brought in by the sweep rakes, and there never was a stacker horse or team without a child on them, two children, three, four children on them, climbing their legs, sitting in rows on their backs, standing to show off when the grown-ups weren't watching; never a stacker horse could there be without a child riding them back and forth and dreaming a million cowboy dreams while they grabbed the hames and rode on the broad warm backs in the early summer sun.

The stacks grow slowly, packed layer on layer, and when they are finally high enough to be soft the children move from the horses to the stacker, riding it up and over and back to drop into the soft hay, bounding and bouncing to pack the hay stack on stack until all the fields are cut for all the families and all the hay is raked and in stacks and each barn is full of new hay, the loft packed for the winter and a different place to play.

And another line.

With haying done there is not a separation of work. It continues. Always. But there is another line to cross and a new time comes then, comes then to the seasons—high summer. Meteorological data mean nothing, technological names mean nothing; the divisions are like music, like stops in a symphony. First thaw, early spring, breakup, middle spring, late spring, early summer, midsummer, high summer, late summer, early fall, Indian summer, first killing freeze, high fall, late fall, first snow, early winter, midwinter, high winter, late winter, first thaw, early spring, breakup . . . more names than months, more names than days, more names because more names are needed. For the luck.

Don't plant potatoes, corn, wheat by the day, by the week, by the month—plant by the moon and the split in the seasons.

Don't castrate lambs, calves, horses by the hour or the doctor but with the moon, the pull of the moon, the silvery dance of the moon.

And so when haying is done it is high summer and the new time comes, the line is crossed and the men look at the hay in the fields in the round stacks in the soft sun and the grain is growing well if the luck is right and the corn is waist high and the equipment is all working and they take a breath and a chance and say:

"What the hell, let's go to the dance Saturday night."

It takes forever, waiting for Saturday. All the time in the world. Each day of work drags, pulls, never ends, each day a year, two days a decade, dragging and dragging until at last the worst day, the longest day, Saturday, and then, finally, it is afternoon and the week, the year, the lifetime is done.

The preparation is in many ways more important than church. The Saturday night ritual. A dressing of toreadors takes less. Chores are—so rare as to shock the system—done early, before daylight is gone, and a quick supper is eaten, sometimes standing while waiting a turn at the hand pump in the kitchen sink. It is a different clean, not like Sunday. Sunday is a soft moving time, a time of spirit and gentleness. Saturday night is raw and the cleaning is a tearing at the dirt, get it done, out of sight, get the clean shirt on and clean overalls and out the door to wait in the back of the truck for the grown-ups to come—and wait and wait and wait until at last they leave the house and the men spit and scratch where the clean shirt itches and the women are fresh and starched, everything is at last perfect and the truck is moving.

To town.

Beer hall, saloon, café—all names for the same place. Where the dance will be. It had once been a storage shed, granary, dry-goods store, town hall—had always once been something else but now it was this, a place for this meeting, this great and raw alive romping, drinking, laughing, puking, crying stomping loving hating wondrous wondrous bastard of a summer dance.

Inside on one wall there is a plank bar where a man sells two things: soda pop and beer in tall dark bottles. They are kept in a metal stock tank full of cool water because there isn't refrigeration and the beer bottles are always wet and running with water but never quite cold, just cool, a tease of cold. No glasses, no cups, no food, no other thing there but the beer in bottles and the soda pop and only two kinds. Orange and grape soda that leaves a stain on your tongue and your lips.

On the other wall there are booths made of rough boards and cushioned with bits of canvas to cover the splinters. At one end of the room there is a board platform for the band.

Band.

One man with a guitar, another with a fiddle, and one man with an accordion.

But not to play yet. The dancing doesn't start right away because the band isn't lubricated properly.

First there is the lubrication. That's what the men call it. Let's get lubed.

The men stand at the plank bar and drink beer from the tall brown bottles with the water running down the sides and the women go to the booths and sit four and six to a booth and laugh and talk and look now and then to the men, and the children divide the same only in different places. The girls form a group along one wall and giggle and point at the boys and the boys stand near the other wall and fight shyness, oh God, fight the shyness that makes them stand looking at the floor when the girls look at them. They drink grape pop holding the bottles like the men, scratch their necks like the men, and go to the cans on the floor and spit like the men and when nobody is looking try to roll corn husk cigarettes like the men until, finally, everything is ready and the men in the band are lubed and the music starts.

Not soft music this, not at first, not music to woo the heart or soul, not music to stir the limp spirit of a poet, not soft and sissy music this but music to stomp by, music to shake the earth by, music to, by God, farm and paw the earth by the band plays.

Reels and schottisches they play, almost in tune but with a grand solid beat that makes the guts jiggle and the feet slam into the floor to raise dust and sweat and then they dance, oh yes don't they dance.

The women fly. Reel and hang on and fly, their skirts out and their laughter whirling around them like jewelry made of silver sound while the men work seriously, their jaws set, work at the music and this business of dancing like they work at farming, at living, at their luck.

Work to the music until their shirts are soaked with sweat and they must stop for another cool bottle of brown beer and a spit in the can—sometimes while the woman waits on the floor—and then back, back to whirl the woman with her skirt flying and her cheeks red and her laughter mixing with the music.

Boys, young boys, red-faced boys finally work up the courage to ask the girls to dance and they do stiff, painful, awkward motions around the floor, sweating not with work but with embarrassment, step-one-two step-one-two.

Older boys still not men are outside. Not dancing but courting and drinking first beers and using their new low voices and trying to make their necks and shoulders thicker while they show off for the young women who come to stand on the steps and sass and tease until two of the boys still not men will fight, do fight; torn shirts, bloody noses, curses, loud grunts and rolling in the dirt and bellows like bulls in the fall.

Saturday night.

Until it is late. Later than any other night and the band has stopped the stomping music and is doing slow waltzes for the men and women who truly love, truly work and truly starve and truly laugh and truly cry and truly love each other; for them the band plays slow waltzes while the children sleep in a booth and the boys still not men sit with girls on the steps and hold hands and touch arms and trade small kisses and large promises and the men and women who truly love waltz with each other slowly around the wooden floor as if the world, the dirt, the animals, the farm, the luck—as if none of it were there. Just their love and the slow waltz in the quiet building with the wooden floors until finally, finally the music stops and the children are carried to the back of the truck still sleeping to drive slowly, slowly home and to bed.

Saturday night.

High summer brings thick heat and there comes a day when dust itches the skin, when the flies and the gnats and the no-see-ums and the thick, humid air and the heat that presses down all build together so that sweat doesn't help, shade doesn't help, and somebody says something about going swimming, just a word, and it becomes the only thing in the world. By the middle of the day work is impossible, everything is impossible but going down to the creek. There is a place, always a place, a special place where the current rounds a bend and goes through a double culvert under the road, and right there, right in that special place the water has dug out a great hollowed pool. Green, green deep to soft brown cool with speckled minnows fleeing from the great splashing monsters who tumble, fall, dive, cannonball from the heavens into the cool clean clear water.

Clothes hanging on the willows, dust hanging on the willows, dirt and grime and work hanging on the willows while the water takes them, takes them all. Skin tightens, pulls in, puckers.

"I can stand on my head under water."

"You're too chicken."

"I can somersault."

"You're yellow clean through."

"I can swim across under water."

"I can dive . . ."

Up on the road over the culverts, six, eight feet, ten feet, a thousand feet down to the water, so high the swimmers look like ants to stand, stand like a pale statue puckered and tight over the pool, over the culverts, over all the world and feel the fear, the fear of failure, of not being able to dive . . .

"Girls are coming!"

. . . to turn and see them, giggling, coming down the road, giggling and pointing at the nakedness, and to dive not in courage but in embarrassment, to dive away from nakedness down and down into the pool and four, six, eight boys jamming into the culverts to hide while the girls stand up on the road and tease and point and sass.

The swimming hole.

Somebody brings the tractor down, the old Minneapolis Moline with the steel lug wheels, and backs it up to the edge of the deep part of the pool. The spring seat, steel with holes in it and stuck on a piece of spring steel like a car spring, the spring seat becomes a perfect diving board and even the men come, bouncing, jumping higher and higher on the seat like great birds to splash in the water.

And a picnic.

At the middle of high summer comes the Fourth of July and there is a picnic. Not the social picnic at the church which comes later and not the family gatherings that come later but the first picnic where not only luck of weather and crops is celebrated but the other luck, luck about where to live. As with the swimming there is a place, a special place down in back of the pasture where the stream winds through and the cows haven't stomped everything into muck. The picnic place. After morning chores and after one of the men goes out on the porch and fires the rifle into a stump—just one shot, not to waste bullets needed later for hunting or slaughtering, one shot into a stump to celebrate the many shots that it took to make a place to live, a place not like the old country. After the shot everybody carries sacks and baskets and blankets down to the special place by the pasture.

To eat. Not like later, not like in the fall when eating becomes something more than eating, becomes fuel, becomes a religion, a contest with God, but to eat on the Fourth of July

41

picnic there is a time when it is fun to eat. Not eat to work, but to have fun.

Potato salad with pepper and fried chicken left to cool in the springhouse, chickens killed and plucked the day before, four, five whole chickens breaded in cornmeal and flour and cooked in full-bodied rendered lard or bear grease from last fall's hunt to make a taste . . . a taste alone. Fresh radishes and green onions and wrinkle-lettuce from the kitchen garden—the only vegetables yet ripe—looking exactly the same as the pictures on the seed packages and in the seed catalog, the radishes red as lips, the onions as green as fresh hay, sitting in pump water in jars with Kerr on the side and metal canning lids, crisp and new and tasting of the earth, almost sweet, and apple pie afterward with crisp crust made with clean lard and sifted flour and little fork holes to let the steam out, apple pie with green apples and sugar and cinnamon so good the fork and the pan must be licked when all the pie is gone.

All afternoon to eat in the special place down at the back part of the pasture, to lie beneath the see-through green leaves of the poplars and eat until movement is impossible and then to close the eyes, let them fall and slip away with a full belly—not stomach but belly—until the sun is starting to go and one of the men rolls a Bull Durham cigarette and smokes it and says:

"Well . . ."

Not ever more, not ever a finished sentence like "well we

have to get back" or "well it's time to do chores" or "well we should think about work." Just:

"Well . . ."

And it's over then. The picnic, Fourth of July, high summer—it's over with that word, that one word:

"Well . . ."

Still before fall, before the killing work of fall, there are summer things to care for, to do.

The garden.

But not one, not just a simple garden but almost a separate farm, a separate life. There are four gardens, four completely different plots. The potato garden, the corn garden, the kitchen garden, and the garden garden.

They are life. More than the farm, more than the crops and the animals, the gardens are life—all food. There is never money, not ever, not even small bits of change, not one extra dime to waste and food from stores—"store boughten"—is simply too expensive except for flour, sugar, salt and pepper, and canning spices. It is unthinkable to buy meat or potatoes or other produce, totally outside thought.

And so the gardens.

An aunt called them the soul of the farm, said the fields of the farm were the body and the house the head and the garden the soul, and she would go out each morning after chores and breakfast, before dishes and day work, and walk through the rows with a cup of steaming coffee held with both hands and talk to the gardens—not wasted talk, not silly talk, but talk as she would speak to another person.

"I was thinking last night of grandmother's quilt," she would say to the cucumber plants. "She used the colors so well. I thought I would try such a quilt, just try and see if I could make it look as pretty as she did . . ."

And nobody laughed, not even a smile, because the garden was as much a part of the family as the people, so important that it was worked separately from the rest of the farm.

A bed in the winter—the gardens were covered with clean straw before first snow and slept snugly, covered all winter until thaw. The small garden, the kitchen garden for lettuce, radishes, green onions, and greens to be worked first, the straw turned under with a shovel and the soil raked and cleaned until it was like black flour and the seeds planted by hand with precision as scientific as any brain surgeon. There was nothing haphazard about any of it. The seeds were sent for in the early spring and when they came plants were started in the house so that every window was filled with tomatoes and eggplants and cabbages and cauliflowers and when it was finally warm enough to plant them outside pages from last year's Sears catalog were used to make frost cones for each tiny plant.

"They get hit when you put them in the soil," they said. "Hard, they get hit. The cold dirt, the cold air, the nights alone after being with us in the house. The paper helps them until they get used to it."

Each day it is necessary to go out and open the paper and let the sun or rain in, then close it again at night, until the paper is tattered and nearly gone and the plants are toughened so that their stalks are hard and green and full.

A year came when there was frost in every month except July and midnights when it was still and frost was smelling close, everybody would be up and out barefoot in underwear covering plants with straw and paper and feed sacks while breath showed and the moon turned all into dancing blue-white ghosts.

Potatoes were everything. Planted with the moon in cushioned rows, dirt pulled up on them all summer to make the right beds, there can be nothing, ever, to compare with new red potatoes as big as a circle with thumb and forefinger; brand new from the hot summer dirt, pulled out sideways so the plant won't know and taken in to be cleaned and boiled with the skin on and served with fresh churned butter and coarse salt and pepper, served with small strips of venison fried in strained rendered oil. It is impossible to stop eating them until they are gone. Until the pan is empty and the butter and meat juices are wiped up with fresh bread and it is not possible to move and the feeling won't come again until next year, the first new potato meal feeling. There will be many other good meals, and good potatoes, white potatoes because they store in the root cellar better and last all winter and red potatoes because they taste better but only once a year, once a year are there new potatoes.

And rhubarb. At the corners of the gardens are the rhubarb plants. They come earlier than the other plants and everybody says they are poison but as soon as the stalks are well up the children cut them and run around sucking them, sucking the pucker-juice from them and nobody gets sick. First new plant from the summer gardens is the rhubarb and as quick as the stalks are big as a thumb it is cut and chopped and made into sauce with sugar to make pies or just to eat from a bowl with a spoon with perhaps three or four canned plums floating in the bowl of sauce. A bite, then a little time for the sugar to work past the sour, then another bite. Radishes, green onions, lettuce, and rhubarb. First summer plants.

The gardens are weeded by hand. Each weed is an enemy. A little hoe made with a tooth of sickle blade hammer-welded to the shank becomes a spear, a sword, a way to deal death and the death dealing, the weeding, is endless, a ritual, a cause.

"If you're just going to sit, go out and weed the garden."

The children are afraid to be seen still, static. If they are not moving, working or seeming to work the voice comes:

"That hand will fit a hoe. It's leaning against the garden fence."

Soon, with all the hands working there are no weeds, not

a tendril, not a sprout. Beans grow as high as a man can reach, sweet corn seems to jump from knee to chest to head and higher, tomatoes become a jungle of thick stalks and rich leaves, and then come the insects. Potato bugs, things that crawl to kill tomatoes and beets and white moths to stick worms in cabbages and each of them, each and every single worm or bug is summarily executed until there seems to be a death zone around the gardens, a place where weeds and bugs cannot live. The gardens, more than other parts of the farm, more than machinery, more than life itself, become a product of complete control; nothing is allowed to interfere and they flourish, more than flourish, become wild jungles of growth, of life, of food.

Nothing is like the first new potato dinner, but close, close comes the first fresh corn on the cob with freshly made butter and gritty salt and mail-order pepper or a tomato taken from the vine when the adults aren't watching and eaten while the heat of the sun is still in it, fresh and dusty warm, or new peas so sweet they're like candy, eaten as fast as they can be picked.

Gardens.

And right after gardens, or during them, comes the time for berries. Raspberries, blueberries, chokecherries, Juneberries, blackberries.

Start picking right after morning chores. Pick and eat and pick and eat and more berries at first hit the mouth than hit the tin lard pail but soon it grows, the pile of berries grows and one pile is added to another until milk buckets are full, so heavy the top berries are mashing the bottom berries into syrup and in the morning there can be pancakes with fresh berry syrup so tangy it's almost like rhubarb.

Stories—berry stories come during berry picking time. Always bear stories. Once Eunice was picking with her sister Esther and she heard a noise on the other side of the bush and thought it was Esther and said for Esther to stop fooling around and finally threw a pebble at her and it wasn't Esther. A bear stood up and snorted so close it blew snot on Eunice who dropped her berry bucket and ran all the way home. And still, when she tells it, her cheeks get red and she snorts like a bear and swears remembering the fear and anger: damn bear, acting like he owns the berries. Another time a bear chased Emily from the berry patch to the wagon, around the wagon back to the house across the pasture, but Emily was gaining at the end and when she hit the porch grabbed the shotgun and those are his claws, there, hanging on the nail on the porch wall by the shotgun. Berry stories always have happy endings: the bear never wins, always just misses, just scares, just chases, just loses, just dies.

There comes a fuzzy time then, when the berry picking mixes with the end of hay gathering and the beginning of late summer and everything seems to fall into a stew. Dog days, when the dog literally will not move from beneath the porch and the weather comes down hot and muggy so the teams of horses stand in sweat even when they are not working.

Right then, when it's impossible to breathe and get out of the heat, right then it is necessary to start canning.

The wood stove in the kitchen must be fired and made hotter than even in the winter, fired with oak and birch and maple mixed until it nearly glows red and the kitchen becomes, truly, hell. There is no air movement and on the first day of canning by midday it is found that the heat in the kitchen is one hundred and twenty, one hundred and thirty degrees on the feed store thermometer on the wall near the calendar with the picture of the smiling girl standing next to a holstein bull. The heat mixes with the steam from the boiling canner until it cannot be borne and then, when breathing is impossible and nothing can live in the kitchen, then at last it is ready and canning can start.

It is all—all food for the winter must be canned. It is everything important. There is not another way to store it—except onions and potatoes and some root crops in the basement. But corn, beets, beans, peas, berries, meat, fruit, tomatoes—all must be canned.

Nobody misses the work. Every ear of corn must be shucked and cleaned and cooked and the kernels shaved off with the corn knife, and if there isn't work in the fields and the gardens are weeded and the chores are done and for some insane reason everybody is not asleep or passed out they must can. They *must* can.

It is when strength shows, canning. Grace, it is said, comes from equal portions of strength and self-denial and somehow, in the kitchen during canning, somehow there is that strength and self-denial and the beauty of grace.

A grandmother and a mother and a daughter all working together. In the evenings on a quilt, sitting on the screen porch their hands close together so it is possible to see the young hands that will become the beautiful old hands, stitching, pulling, stitching . . .

And in the kitchen it is the same. The same three. But hard now, the work. Hot beyond belief and filled with steam and peelings and ends of beans and the piles of vegetables or meat to cook and can. The grandmother leaning over a pot of cucumbers to pickle, the mother working at string beans, the daughter to be a mother to be a grandmother, the daughter helping with the beans all in steam and perspiration so their dresses stick to them and their hair is matted to their heads. And in all that, in all that heat and pots and pans banging around and steam, there is laughter; constant, teasing laughter.

"Billy danced with you Saturday night, didn't he? During the slow dancing?"

"Oh, Mama—that doesn't mean anything."

"It always means the same thing. Means he's sparking for you and will come courting."

"Nobody does that anymore. Comes courting—that's old-fashioned."

"Some things never change—there'll come a soft late summer night and he'll come to help shuck corn and one thing will come to the next and you'll be in the back of the barn with him, stealing a kiss, stealing a kiss, stealing a kiss . . ."

Laughter mixed with steam and heat and sweat and a hand to come up and push the gray hair back from a temple that wasn't always gray and the vegetables and meat pour into the jars marked Kerr and Mason with the galvanized lids and real rubber seal rings that can be shot from a thumb and forefinger. Meat and vegetables and fruit in jar after jar after jar to line the root cellar shelves down the small hole in the kitchen floor; a flood of jars to fill the shelves and every corner and nook and it doesn't seem to end.

As with other work. There never seems to be an end to canning except that one day in the late summer, in the late late summer the kitchen is normal again and it can't be remembered just when it happened. There is peace and the air is fresh and the steam is gone and the canning is in some way finished and nobody saw it end.

And there is a pause.

A small pause and then a flurry of late summer work to be done. Equipment to be mended, always that, but now everything must be checked and rechecked to prepare for the hard run of fall work. Harnesses again, oiled and stitched if they are loosened, wheels on wagons greased and the horses' hooves cleaned and trimmed and shod if necessary and the horses must be wormed with tobacco. Two medicines for stock—

tobacco and Corona udder balm salve—and one medicine for people, cod-liver oil. So awful that the young stay well out of fear.

Plow blades and hay sickles to be greased and pulled into the shed next to the barn until next year, mousetraps to be placed in the granaries and house and checked and rechecked as the mice come in at the end of summer to make their homes for winter. The traps are deadly and yield sometimes thirty, forty mice a day until they stop their inward migration, which comes at the end of each summer.

Leaks to be patched and boards to be replaced in the barns and granary walls and fence . . .

Always the fence to be mended.

The bull has pushed here and the cows have pushed there and the wire must be restretched and renailed and with the fence come the wire stories—always the wire stories.

There was the time that Nels trained his team to stretch wire and made a bracket to pull three strands at once and hold them. It was slick, slick as a new calf. He would stretch half a forty of wire, hook the team to it and they would take up the strain and hold it tight like fiddle strings while Nels went back down the wire and stapled it to the posts. But one day the team stepped in a nest of ground hornets and they drove the team mad with stinging while Nels was halfway back on the wire and they lunged and the wire snapped and whipped back and cut Nels's head off clean as an axe. Killed him dead, right there and his wife didn't come and find him until she saw the team out in the alfalfa dragging wire and harness chain. Broke her heart, the poor thing, and she never married again and raised her boy to go to work in the city.

Wire stories. Like hay stories and berry stories with sadder endings. Wire stories never have happy endings.

Wire snapped and took his leg off, his arm, goddamn barb-wire, snapped and went back and killed their baby on the wagon; wire snapped and went back, went back and opened him like a hog cut for gutting; stretched and went back and around his eyes and blinded him for life. Goddamn wire.

Comes a day then, in the hot times of the late summer, when right after church instead of eating the big meal, food is put in milk buckets wrapped in dish towels and coffee is put in jars wrapped with paper and feed sacks and cane poles are tied to the top of the old truck.

There is a place, another special place where the river makes a bend, one, two miles over past Gustafson's place, down around a corner by a cattail swamp or is it just where the road dips over the creek by those big culverts they put in four years back—just there, just . . . some . . . place . . . right . . . there is a hole and it's filled with sunfish, crappies, bream, rock bass bullheads catfish bluegills.

And they're waiting, just waiting, to jump on a hook. Blankets are spread and the food is taken out and put on the blankets and the buckets are filled with cool water from the river and fishing is begun. Worms are the bait, or grasshoppers, or parts of the first fish caught are cut away and used, and there is art to it, serious art, as serious as any art there ever was or will be. The poles, whether held by adults or children, must be held a certain way and the lines swung out and dropped with little hooks and pinch-tab sinkers and corded nylon black line with wire leaders. The lines must swing out in a gentle arc, then drop back into the water and be allowed to fall naturally, and if nothing bites on the first attempt it is done again, and again.

Serious fishing while sitting in the sun and each fish is dropped in the bucket if it is big enough, as big as a man's hand, as big as the top of a boy's head, as big as a girl's face, as big as Grandma's smile. Each fish kept there, cool and alive, until two, three buckets are full with dozens of fish and the Sunday sun has everybody lazy and ready to sleep and the heat has stopped the fish biting.

Then home to the eager cats and the dog who know what is coming. In back of the barn a factory line is set up. One to snap the head with the knife to kill them, cut the head off and slice the guts out, as neat as any doctor, and throw the heads and guts to the yowling-mowling cats and jumping whining dog, then another to use a kitchen spoon or three bottlecaps nailed to a piece of board to scale the fish, scales flying into hair and onto faces.

All of it, from dead to meat back in a bucket of cool water, not taking over ten seconds and when all the fish are cleaned and the cats and dog so full they cannot move, back to the house with the fish. Forty, fifty of them to dip in cornmeal-egg-flour batter and fry in butter and lard mixed with salt and pepper while the tail raises and curls and turns crunchy until the skin just lifts crisp and steaming. Pan after pan while new potatoes boil and then to the table. Just fish and potatoes with perhaps onions and radishes and they must be eaten then. Right then. Even if evening chores are due the fish and potatoes must be eaten and the skeletons left on a side plate to be burned because they will choke the dog and cats and even the pigs can't have them.

Fish after fish, alive and then minutes later on the table with salt and pepper and butter, forty, fifty of them to eat until nobody can move.

But must. Must move to go and milk, do evening chores so full it's hard to walk, to bend, and even the bib overalls are pushed out with it.

Late summer and one more thing that always seems to come before fall, just after the heat and before school and when there is that pause, that time that cannot be measured.

First love.

Always then it seems to come. Perhaps it started at the dance or in church or at the store in town, just started there but the summer makes it grow as it makes all things grow and by late summer it is there, first love. She is this and she is that, he is that and he is this, the sun rises and sets on her hair, he can move a mountain, the moon in her eyes, his hands can circle her waist—all talk, all thinking is of her, of him, of them. He walks four miles after chores just to sit on the porch with her and stammer his heart, stammer his soul, and she must read love in phrases like: It is a good night; the corn rustles as it grows; have you ever seen such nice weather? And he must find his life, his reason to live in her lowered eyes, her touch on his arm, the way the soft hair at her temples looks in the moonlight. Many times it is not asked, the question, and not given, the answer; perhaps most times it is not asked and not given. They talk for a time and she knows that he cannot ask it, cannot make the words in his mind let alone make them come through his mouth and into the air; is so shy it can *not* come. But she knows, and he knows, and they do not need to ask and answer because it is late summer and in that time almost nothing has to be said.

High summer, late summer doesn't end, never ends until one day when all the hay is up and all the canning is done and all the first meals are eaten and all the true first loves have been declared and one day the same man who tasted the soil, one day he walks to the oat field or the barley field or the wheat field alone.

He has walked there every day for a week, every day for two weeks, sometimes twice a day and sometimes in the evening when the chores are done, he has walked there. He has stood there every day, watched the field every day, smelled the field every day, listened to the field and, finally, on this day he will roll a cigarette with Bull Durham from the little cloth sack or fill his lip with snuff from the little round can after tapping the lid with a calloused thumb. He will smoke the cigarette or spit the snoose after a bit and then lean down and cup heads of grain in his hands. The hands roll the grain in a gentle rubbing motion, the way he might touch a new calf or a baby, and he will open the hands and blow the chaff away softly, a kiss of breath, a kiss, and he will look at the grain cupped in his hand and nod, a slow nod and say: "It's time."

And it is fall.

FALL

ALL WORK, ALL THE WORK THERE IS OR HAS BEEN IS FOR THIS now, all has been leading up to this time, this fall, and now luck, all the luck must come as well.

If this does not go well, if this fails then everything for the spring and summer is for nothing.

Harvest.

So clean a word, so neat a word for what must come, for what must be.

As with the haying, families work together. There is one threshing machine to be taken around to several farms. One great monster of a galvanized beast of a machine with wheels and levers and belts and chains all to separate the small head of grain from the plant—just this one part of fall is so difficult it almost cannot be.

They talk of how it used to be—the old-timers. Old Gustaf

and Uncle David and Ole and Otto and Swen—they talk of how it was before there were threshing machines.

Grain brought in sheaves on wagons to be beaten with wooden flails and, by God, that was when men were men; they could work a scythe and cradle all day, sharpened on a whetstone so sharp it was like a razor, cut grain all day so smooth it fell before it knew it was cut and then come in and work the flail until past dark, past dark, and then get out the fiddle and dance all night—Goddamn, *that* was when men shook the earth. None of this weak business with the threshing machines, by God, but *work* . . .

And yet.

And yet now when the work of threshing begins it is hard to see how it could be worse, how the work could be harder.

The threshing machine is pulled into place on the back side of the farm, settled and hunkered in like a hungry beast—enormously mechanical, mysterious—and the old F-12 or Minneapolis Moline or John Deere tractor is brought into place in front of the machine, away from the machine but connected by an umbilical belt, a great thirty or forty foot belt from the flywheel of the tractor and twisted—always twisted and why is that?—twisted to go around another wheel on the threshing machine.

To sit. To sit while men come like nurses to care, to love and care for the quiet waiting beast. They have oil cans and grease guns and they oil and grease and tighten and tune, a nut here, a lever there, smiling and spitting and taking last sips of coffee from jars. There is that time, that moment before work and the boys mimic the men, standing with their hands in their overall pockets, spitting and nodding and wiping grease off the grease serts with their thumbs until one of the men or maybe two of them nod and say:

"Let her rip."

She—it is always she—doesn't start easy. The clutch on the tractor is eased in, out, back in while the mysterious inner workings of the threshing machine, the grills and grates and shakers and blowers, all take up the slack and begin to moan, the guts begin to heave.

It is, always, a marvel—more than any other mystery-dance on the farm the threshing machine is a marvel.

Around it, eyes worried, hands moving with grease guns and oil cans, loving hands, dirty hands, anxious hands—around the huge silver monster the men hover.

"Goddamn, I should have replaced that keyway—the grate wheel is slipping."

But it holds, oh yes it holds, and the grates begin to shuffle back and forth, the small saw teeth ripple like water, oh yes, the keyway holds and the machine—she—groans and heaves and humps and bucks and in a great crashing of noise and year-old dust and mouse nests it is there. It is there. Where there was only cold steel and shafts and arms and still gears now—now there is life. Now, by God, there is a threshing machine.

Still there is worry.

"Goddamn grease might be dry on the auger shaft." Swear—always swear and always spit and always put wrists and hands up through the suspenders on the bib overalls but always, always swear. "Son of a bitch squeals like a pig on that down stroke. I'll bet the goddamn grease cup is dry . . ."

Noise. Thundering noise roars and clanks from the threshing machine—noise and dust and finally a smile, two smiles in dirty greasy faces and a new lip full of snoose to spit from and someone says:

"Hell—let's thresh some grain."

Before this, before this each day the swatters have been working to shock the grain.

When they talk, when the old-timers talk of how it used to be when men walked with scythes, and when they talk of that they sometimes come to that place where they saw their first swatter, their voice trails, ends in a breath and they say:

"It come on a week in summer, come to Holt on the train and you should have seen her. I never seen the beat of it. So many gears and levers and chains Pa he said it couldn't work—would just fall apart."

They breathe, a long breath, a breath to power stories.

"Come with a book, full of pictures this book, and he worked a by-God week to get it together. First time he hooked it to a team I thought they'd tear it to pieces and, oh Christ, didn't he fly?"

It was the first machine, the first time a man, a walking breathing man, could be replaced by a machine, and they spoke with their voices down, almost a whisper.

"Shocked twenty acres in a day—we had to pull Pa off the damn thing."

The grain must come to the threshing machine. It must come in love, must come in all gentleness or the heads will fly loose and be lost.

And so the binder. The swatter. The shocker. They are all the same—a device so wondrous that even after the old days, even after tractors and bigger tractors and echelons of combines to thresh forty acres an hour, even after all the new marvels there are, an uncle goes out behind the barn where the rusting binder lies and puts his hand on it the way he might put his hand on a favorite cow and says:

"Come that first year when we got the binder I thought hell, we could farm the world."

And it was this way with the swatter. Horses pulled it and a ribbed driving wheel worked the machinery. A man sat above the wheel and drove the team.

At the front edge of the reaper—yet another name—was a sickle bar with cutting blades that whirred as they did on a hay mower and cut the grain. But instead of falling on the ground the cut grain was pushed back on a moving canvas belt by rotating wooden paddle blades, flashing like sun through honey each time they passed. The canvas belt carried the grain into a twine binder that gathered bunches of it, tied it off with twine, and dumped it back on the ground.

Exactly—it had to happen exactly right, cut the grain too soon and it is not loose enough for the threshing machine to separate the head from the plant, too late and the heads will fall off when the shocks are moved.

And rain will kill it all. Rain now, with the grain on the ground will ruin the grain, cause it to swell and try to replant itself, and hail will knock it all loose to be lost in the dirt.

That's how they say it. "Lost in the dirt." It is not soil then, nor earth, nor the land but just dirt and to lose it in the dirt, to have all the work of all the year turn sour because of rain or hail or even winds that are too strong, to have it all be for nothing and be lost in the dirt is the worst thing there is, the worst of all.

A man follows the reaper on foot with a fork and he gently gathers the shocks, five or six of them, and stands them against each other, leans them like friends to be picked up later when it is time to thresh. When it is time.

Now.

The machine runs and continues to run and men take hay-racks pulled by teams to the fields and load them high, impossibly high with stacks of shocks that come lumbering in next to the threshing machine where they are forked into a chute with a chain belt that drags the shocks down past a man who cuts the twine off and then into the machine.

Into it as sheaves of grain, tumbling yellow in the sun, and there the miracle that is never seen, the inner workings of the threshing machine miracle takes place.

There are two chutes leading away from the machine. One is a blower and out of this blower comes a constant stream of straw and chaff and dust so thick that within moments, seconds, it is not possible to see or breathe around the machine. The men put bandannas around their mouths and squint and rub their eyes but nothing helps and soon their eyes are red, blood red, and their faces are so covered with dust they crack when the men smile, teeth white in the clouds of dust, and they smile, always during threshing they smile not because of the straw chute but because of the other, the grain auger.

It stands like a totem from the side of the threshing machine, high and out to the side to be lowered over a waiting grain wagon, held by a team of horses that stand next to the machine, their feet moving nervously, frightened of the noise and the dust and the slapping belt from the old tractor to the drive wheel of the machine.

Belt stories are like pig stories and wire stories.

"It was Legarrd, didn't think what he was doing and the belt caught his shirt, pulled his arm from the socket and tore it clean off to where it thumped around the drive wheel."

Or a child, always a child. "They didn't watch the baby over to Nelsons and he wandered into the belt, pulled him into the flywheel on the tractor and there wasn't nothing come out you could call human. The woman was never the same, never the same . . ."

But the auger, the grain auger that stands over the waiting wagon, that is what people watch. It is impossible to not watch it, the auger because here it will come, here it will come.

The grain.

It is a trickle at first. Almost single kernels and then half cups as the auger spurts them up and out the top of the auger chute and tumbling down into the empty wooden grain wagon where a child, always a child for this and for the tops of haystacks, where a child waits with a shovel almost as big as he is, a huge grain scoop.

And it comes.

That little bit comes and then the shocks begin feeding into the threshing machine faster, one on top of another and another, tumbling off the hayracks and into the feed chute and past the twine cutter and down into the guts of the machine and the grain becomes a small stream, then a river, a river of gold pouring from the top of the auger tube into the wagon, which isn't called a wagon but a grain tank.

Gold.

Rich, pouring, a river of gold as grand as the cream that comes from the separator is the wheat or barley or oats, and the dust and noise and itching and red eyes are forgotten in that river of richness coming out of the tube and there will be much of it, so much that the boy in the wagon will be hard pressed to stay ahead of the river, scooping the grain away to even the load, so much if the luck is right that wagon after wagon will heave with it but it will always be something fine, that gold, that flow of grain.

And each man and each woman will find some way to come and touch it, feel it, hold a hand under the downpour or push a hand and arm down into the load in the wagon. Each will do it. To hell with the thistles and grasshoppers that come through the threshing machine and mix with the grain. They will come to touch it. And many will do it more than once, come and feel the gold, watch the gold, and each time they do it, feel it and watch it, each and every time they will smile.

But it is only part of the harvest dance, that stream, that load of grain, only a small part. The men bring the racks of shocks to the threshing machine from the fields in an endless circle and the machine tears them apart and the straw pile grows until it is higher and wider than the barn, higher and wider than a mountain and still it is not done, the dance. It is only started.

When the wagons are filled, heaping, the teams buckle in and pull them to the granary.

Pressure now. There are only two grain wagons, grain tanks, and one is filling while the other must be emptied.

By hand.

One man starts with a shovel, a grain scoop. A tarp is laid on the ground beneath the granary wall to catch anything that spills and one man starts. He fills the scoop, raises and throws the load through an impossibly small hole that always seems to be higher than is comfortable to throw. A rhythm. Up with the load, around, aim, and just on release lift slightly on the handle to aim the grain into the hole.

And again.

And again.

And it must be faster than the grain coming from the threshing machine into the next wagon or the machine will get ahead and the dance will stop, the dance will stop and the rhythm will be ruined.

The shovel must lower and raise each time and the grain must hit the hole and down again and up and into the hole. With oats, with barley it is bad enough, hard enough, but wheat and flax are heavy, so heavy they will break a man trying to keep up with the machine and so two men are used. Because the tank is narrow, only four feet between sides, there is only room for one man to work at a time and when the heat cooks him down or his back cannot stand it longer still he goes, still he works, and when he has gone past the point where he should have stopped he finally moves and the other man steps in to pick up the rhythm.

Some never straighten again fully after shoveling flax or wheat. Some walk always forward a little, always with the stoop, always bent to the grain for the rest of their lives or perhaps it is the other things, the other things of work. The horses that lean on them while shoeing or the machinery they must lift, or life, but many say it is the grain. The first time. The grain pulls the muscles along the backbone, the tenderloin muscles they say, pulls them and stretches them so they never come back.

It does not end when the wagon is empty.

There is another wagon.

Cool water hangs on the threshing machine in thick linen water bags with a metal spout and a cork. The water seeps through the linen and evaporates and keeps the water cool and it cannot be more delicious, nothing can be more delicious than a drink from a linen water bag with the cork and metal taste from the spout in the dust and thick heat of threshing. Nothing. The water cuts the chaff and takes the mind away from the work, the shovel, the noise.

For a moment. Cool peace for a moment. The men take that moment to look at the grain, to stand up on the wheel of the grain tank and look down into the load and perhaps push their hand down into the warm richness before returning to work.

Then back to it, back to the stream of gold from the auger,

back to the endless roar of the machine and the blowing straw and that wonderful pouring rich flow and soon there is nothing else.

When it stops for the day, when it finally stops, it is not because of any conscious decision, not because of exhaustion, which drives everybody, all things. If a machine breaks, the tractor or thresher, it is fixed rapidly with much cursing and spitting and work resumed often in minutes, to continue as long as wire and spit will hold. Horses get so tired from the wagons and pulling the hayracks and the heat and the dust that they weave when they stand and sometimes go down, back end first and then the front, only to be pulled up. They are grained and watered where they stand, salt rubbed inside their lips so they'll drink more water, water poured on them to cool them down but still to work, to keep working. Men drop, sometimes sit or take small breaks leaning against a wheel or the side of a wagon, but the machine, the wonderful rich beautiful goddamn machine keeps going and they must feed it until . . .

Dew.

It is dew that decides.

Sun, dryness are too precious to waste and as long as they last the thresher will run because to deny it, to waste threshing weather is to court, to beg for, failure. Waste it now and they won't give it to you again. Throw it away, waste harvest

72

weather and they—always "they"—will take it from you and it might rain or hail or wind will blow.

But dew. Evening dew can stop it, does stop it. Grain cannot be threshed wet. The heads will rot, heat, sprout in the granary. It must be dry.

Nobody admits to it, nobody will ever admit to it, but there are those who pray for dew, beg in their minds for dew, watch the stems of grass as evening comes and beg inside their thoughts, plead for the droplets to form. But never say it. Not even the children, who sometimes fall asleep beneath the threshing machine, not even the men who lean on the side of the grain wagon and cannot straighten from the shoveling, young men, men who have necks like bulls and laughs like thunder, bend as with age, bend and hang on the side of the wagon with moist eyes from the pain—even they will not say it. But it is there, the soft prayer for dew.

And it comes.

It always comes. Before dark but after pain there comes the soft dampness and somebody—who will be first?—somebody says, yells over the noise of the machine:

"It's getting wet. That's it—cut her down."

And clutches are eased to stop the threshing machine, the tractor is stopped, the dust settles, the teams are unhooked and unharnessed and fed and turned out to roll in the pasture, the last grain is shoveled into the granary, every kernel is cleaned off the tarp, and it is just before dark as everybody troops silently to the house.

To eat.

"There is no pay in farming," the old ones say, almost chant. "There is no pay in farming, but you never starve. There is always food."

Legends are told of threshing meals. As the team moves around from farm to farm, the family at the working farm is responsible to feed the whole crew and it is part of the dance, the eating, the size and quality of the meal.

"It means something," an aunt said, "it means something when they can't get up from the table and the bowls are empty. It means something about who you are when you feed them right."

The women have, if possible, worked harder than the men. Up early, three in the morning, two-thirty, midnight, up to make bread dough to punch down, flour in their hair and up their arms, bread dough to make loaves to wipe hot with butter and sprinkle with a touch of salt and pepper and serve in racks; up early to peel potatoes and soak meat for good gravy; up early to open jars of rhubarb for sauce; up early to peel apples and roll dough and heat the ovens for bread and pie. To cook.

To cook all day. From the dark of early morning through the day with no breaks, to peel and roll and knead and cook. Mothers, sisters, aunts, daughters all working, no matter the age. Side by side. And in laughter, always in laughter, teasing about boys and men and talking of dreams and sadnesses, but always somehow in laughter while they work. Food in small amounts all day. Lunch brought in lard buckets to men while they work, bites to be snatched between shovels full of grain, between loads of shocks, quick food to stay alive; coffee in jars wrapped in feed sacks, swallowed black and hot with thick bread sandwiches and a piece of cake, all eaten by hand, all wolfed.

Until the dew.

The evening meal.

Everyone lines up at a wash bench where pans are set with towels and coarse lye soap. The dirt is thick, fills the water so that just to clean the face and hands, just to make the face a white circle sometimes requires the bowl to be rinsed and refilled three and four times.

Tables are set in the yard, end to end, and in much noise the men come to sit and eat. Feed. Bowls of potatoes and brown gravy and jars with fresh green onions in cool water and radishes from the garden and loaves of bread, nearly one per person, and jars of honey and others with jelly and home-made sweet brown ketchup and plates of meat, roasts and steaks, and pans of rolls to supplement the bread and bowls of cooked corn and string beans . . .

The table sags, groans with it. Sometimes a grace, another prayer for the luck, and then the food is gone.

"You eat," a grandmother says, "like wolves. Just like wolves."

Jaws aching with hunger, bodies past tired, past death, the food is there and then it is gone. A blur of eating. No talk, no words except pass this or hand that, cheeks bulging with it, mouths chewing with it, and the bowls are empty, bread has wiped the last gravy and then the pie comes.

More coffee. Hot from the pot now, black and thick and hot and then pie. Apple or rhubarb or mince or green tomato but mostly apple. Wrinkle-pinched around the edges and sprinkled with sugar and cinnamon, brown to golden with fork holes to let the steam out and little trails of sweet juices from the fork holes.

The pie is religious, something from God. The only part of the meal to be eaten slowly. Huge pieces, a quarter pie per person, and between each bite a drink of coffee and when the pie is done, the fork is held sideways in the hand and swiped around the plate to get the absolute last of the juice and apple and crust.

Then one more cup of coffee. Boxes of sugar cubes are brought to the table and each man takes a cube and dips it in hot coffee until it is just starting to crumble, then puts it in his lower lip where the snuff goes during the day and "sweetens the pocket." Two, three lumps that way, then drink the coffee and it is dark and time to rest.

Some sleep where they are. At the table. Lean forward and sleep. Some on blankets on the porch, some beneath the machinery to keep dew from falling on them, just down and sleep.

But not for long, the sleep, the rest. Almost none for the women. Work starts at first light, four in the morning, and there must be breakfast before that and breakfast is another meal like supper. Never dinner. Dinner is the noon meal. The night meal is supper.

Before light the cows are milked and the extra men come from where they were sleeping to the house. The women have been working since midnight getting food ready.

Coffee.

Pots of coffee. The big old pots with no strainers, none of the soft perk weak coffee or drip grind but coffee boiled in the same pot, boiled by the handful with eggshells thrown in to take the acids out, the smoothest strongest coffee there is.

Coffee first. Cup on cup, wolfed back so hot it sears the mouth and throat, slammed down to bring the new day, to jerk the brain up from sleep.

Then bacon and scrambled eggs and pancakes and gravy and biscuits. Not a choice. Everybody eats all of them, plus raw fried potatoes with pepper on them and thick rhubarb and raspberry sauce on the pancakes so the stomach is tight, drum tight for the start of the day.

Still there is dew. It comes light but there is dew as the men walk stiffly, some stooped, others limping from humping the fork handle with their leg all day to get the shocks higher on the hayracks when loading.

Stooped, limping, filling their lower lips with snoose they

leave the tables and move to the barn and threshing machine to get ready for the day.

Oil cans, grease guns in hand, men descend on the threshing machine and begin fixing her for another day. Grease, rags, shafts, and bearings—a blur of men poking and digging and wiping and greasing. Other men move to the barn and pastures and bring out the teams. They are as stiff as the men and move slowly until they are grained and rubbed and the harness is on them. Some men cool coffee and spit it in the horses' mouths, others mix it in their water. Ponderously they are backed in alongside the tongues on the grain tanks, the tongues are lifted to the collar crosspiece and the trace chains are hooked to the singletrees.

Last Bull Durham cigarettes are rolled and smoked, last lips are filled with snoose, somebody feels the grass and nods.

"It's dry."

The tractor pops, pops again and fires and starts, the clutch is eased slowly in, the machine grunts, squeaks, trembles and it is there again, the noise, the dust, the straw and golden grain.

Not for a day, this—not for two days. However long it takes at one farm, then on to another farm where the work is the same, all the men and all the teams. The women stay at home to milk and do chores while the men move from farm to farm where the only change is the meals. A competition is there, a friendly competition on who can serve the best meal and the men talk about it, tease the women about it.

"Over to Petersons' they had covers on their pies, little lattice work covers to make it look like a fence . . ."

"She had something in the bread, that Mrs. Halverson— maybe it was honey or molasses. Just a taste of sweetness that made you want to keep coming back."

"You could cut the venison with a fork . . ."

And the meals get better all the time, larger, insanely larger and better all the time until there is so much the men can't possibly eat it all without foundering.

But they do. They eat and clean every bowl, every plate, every pie pan at every farm while the work goes on, pushing daylight into dark and dark back into daylight, working until they drop and every crop at every farm is in the granaries.

Harvest.

But only the first part. Hay is a summer crop and the fall harvest begins with the grain, oats, and barley, but there is corn to get in for silage for the cattle and that is more work, though all done on each farm and not by teams that go around. Chopped corn blown into the silage pit next to the barn with a shredder run off the belt of the tractor and there are silage fumes stories. Corn chopper stories.

"He was in the silo, forking it when the fumes overtook him. Nobody thought to look for him all that morning and when they found him he was dead. Said he had a smile on his face . . ."

Silage ferments, gives off a sweet smell to hide the methane in it, the killer gas that floats in silos to kill and explode if a match is lighted.

Corn choppers and shredders are of all machinery the most deadly, the quickest to maim and kill. A toothed chain feeds the corn into a chopper that shreds it and blows it into the silo or silage pit and if it catches somebody it is usually fatal. All families have someone with a finger or thumb gone, quick jerks, a cut and tug, a whirring saw and it is gone, but corn choppers take more, take all, and sometimes there is nothing to bury.

"Over to Engstroms' the young one, I think she was three, fell into the corn chopper and they had to bury silage, she was so mixed in . . ."

Fast—two, three seconds and it's done.

Then the granaries are filled, the silage is up, the hayloft is packed and the stacks are in the fields, the canning is done and the young ones are back in school.

There has been no money. Anything earned belongs to the farm and there is nothing extra, but now the word comes that the potato farms west half a day need pickers and so school closes down and the young ones are released to go pick potatoes.

"Sack spuds," the old ones say, "off like gypsies to pick spuds."

The grown-ups would put gas in the old truck and fill the radiator and check the oil and send off the young ones for school money, clothes money, spending money.

Self money.

Farmers had sacks in granaries for sleeping and served one hot meal a day and sandwiches but nobody slept, nobody rested. The money was too important.

A nickel a bushel here, down the road six cents, over across the section somebody paying seven cents, and rumors that one complete maniac four miles farther out was paying ten cents.

A dime a bushel.

Drive the truck there, hurry, before he changes his mind.

Riches. Arithmetic, figures in the dirt, pick twenty bushels a day and make two dollars. Pick thirty, three dollars. That was man's wages, three a day and found. A good man. Pick thirty a day, and make twenty-four dollars in a week. Twenty-four dollars in a pocket, burning there, in one week, to spend on anything. To spend mostly on school clothes, but some saved for anything. A new knife, new engineer boots or belt or straw cowboy hat or enough candy to make you puke.

"With that much money . . ." They say but can only dream.

A week. It can only be a week because that is all school is closed. Five school days and two weekends and if the fall rains come it's all over. There won't be any picking and no money. Nine days.

Nine days to make dreams come true.

A large digger is pulled through the field by a tractor with steel lug wheels and in back of it the potato row is turned up and over, split open to show the potatoes. Little treasures in the dirt, potatoes to bring money, potatoes to bring riches.

There are no limits on picking except light. It doesn't matter if there's dew or hot sun or wind and payment comes by the bushel. Everybody takes a sack—they're placed in stacks at intervals in the field—and kneels and starts picking.

At first it is even. Everybody starts at the same place in a line, each on his own row, but rows vary and the density of potatoes varies and there is talking at first, and much laughter, but in a short time everybody is separated and the sun cooks down and there is nothing but potatoes.

Each sack a bushel, each sack a dime. The first sack seems to go fast and the mind clicks like a cash register.

A dime.

Nine more sacks and it's a dollar.

The second sack goes well, but a bit slower.

The third slower yet.

Thirty cents.

By the fourth sack, fifth sack, tenth sack fifteenth sack twentieth sack there is no more counting, only the work. Only the spuds, only the spuds and the heavy sack and time stops and life stops and thinking stops and there is only picking.

Everything burns. The back of the neck takes the full brunt of the sun and cooks and blisters and then doesn't matter. Some boys pick without shirts and their backs are not used to the sun and they burn as well, burn and reburn until they are as black as the dirt they kneel in.

Potatoes.

In some part of the day, a middle part but it doesn't matter, there is a sandwich and cold water from a galvanized insulated water container and then picking again until it is so dark it's impossible to see the potatoes, until they can only be found by feeling, and finally even then it is too dark and everybody walks back to the farmyard for food on wooden tables.

But not threshing food, this. Not the huge meals.

Farm worker food is not the same as threshing food. A pot of soup, thin stew, metal plates and day-old store-bought bread from the bakery in town. No coffee. Just cold water. Or beans. Just beans and thin slices of bread with no butter. Sometimes the metal plates are nailed to the table with a roofing nail in the middle of each and when the food is done buckets of hot water are sloshed in them to clean them for the next meal. Big farms, business farms. And sometimes in the next field there are Mexicans from Mexico who came in buses working, whole families working picking potatoes, picking them so fast it doesn't seem possible, working ahead and more ahead of those who pick for money, self money. Always in white, the Mexicans, and always the white against the black dirt looks so clean and fresh and they never seem to get dirty and all wonder how that can be, when they work so hard, so very hard, so very very hard.

Boys and girls are separated at night. Two different granaries with burlap gunny sacks for beds and the first night even with exhaustion new people meet new people and talk into the night, all night.

"Did you see the girl with the long black hair? She had it in a braid that went past her waist."

"I tried picking alongside that guy from Grand Forks and he left me like I was standing still. But he's picking good, even with the speed. He's going to be richer than God . . ."

A day and then another day and by the third day crawling along picking, by the third day there has never been anything else but picking. No families, no homes, no more talking at night, not even any more complaining about the poor food, only picking, only spuds and when the week is done, when the final Sunday comes, the farmer pays off.

Not with checks. Never with checks. Always with cash. He has a cigar box from the house and he comes out with the cigar box and opens it and it is full of money. Each person has kept track of his or her bushels on a piece of paper sacking and the farmer has a notebook with an Indian on the cover where he has also kept a tally and sometimes they match and sometimes they do not.

When they do not match there is arguing but the farmer always wins because he has the money and the farm and the potatoes and all the picker has is a piece of paper sack but there is still money.

"Something for the pocket," an uncle says. "Everybody needs something for the pocket . . ."

The old truck is fired up and everybody piles in for the half-day ride back to the farm, to work, to school, to the rest of fall, but on the way . . .

On the way the truck passes a small store and everybody piles out to drink Nesbitt's orange pop in tall orange bottles wet from a cooler with a lid that raises and to eat Baby Ruth candy bars and to spend some of the money from the pocket before it has to be spent on practical things, on school clothes or new gloves.

There is a sadness to ending picking and a joy and things to tell back at the farm, things about Mexican workers who work harder even than the men during threshing and never get dirty and of girls with hair down their backs and fields of potatoes so large they seem to reach out to the sky, of farms without fences that go on and on, or the prairie sky with no trees to stop it that seems a bowl over everything. Many things to tell and when the truck pulls into the yard it seems to have been a year, a lifetime away, and everybody runs to talk at once, to tell at once, to show at once.

When the harvest of grain and corn is done and the potato picking is done and the canning is done, the weather could go bad, could rain, could do anything but it doesn't. Perversely it remains perfect. Clear dry warm days and cool nights while the leaves change and the color comes.

School starts and there are the new engineer boots rubbed with oil and the new jean jacket and the two new tablets with the Indian on the front the same as the potato farmer had and the wooden pencil box with the sliding top and a special place for the eraser, one end red and the other gray that always tears the pulpy tablet paper. New school days, the first days, even in the old schoolhouse they are still new. Old friends new because they are different in school from how they are in summer, new books to study because it is a new grade. Same room, same teacher, but new.

Walking to school is the same as walking through a painting or a picture on a calendar. Two miles and a little more, hard in winter, miserable in the mud of spring but now it is clear and dry and the color fills the trees, hangs over the road. Golden maples turning to red that almost touch overhead, explosions of yellow from the poplars and red from sumac, so bright it causes a squint when the sun is right, and to walk through it, to walk in it so the color becomes part of the air and can be breathed, to walk in it and breathe the color in new boots and a new jacket with money from potato picking . . .

Sometimes it feels there was never anything before it and there can never be anything after it; that there is only that time, that one rich time in all a life to live, but of course that is not true, there is more.

More to life.

More to fall.

There is killing and more canning.

Nothing runs without meat. That's how they say it, the old ones. Bread is good, but nothing runs without meat and there can be no meat without killing but nobody except the dog and the barn cats like it.

Two pigs must be killed each year and one steer and close on a hundred chickens and for a week and more that is all that can be done.

It always comes slowly, the killing. The weather is too warm or there is machinery to repair and get ready to put down for the winter or it is raining and too wet or it is Sunday and you never kill on Sunday or the Halversons are coming to visit for an afternoon or . . .

Or.

Or.

But at last there is a morning and an uncle is sitting at the kitchen table with a whetstone and a small can of fine oil. The stone is on a piece of paper so dirt will not get on the oilcloth on the table and ruin the printed flowers and he slides a knife with a long curved blade easily across the stone, floating on the oil in a circular motion, a gentle roundabout push and slide that turns the knife into a razor, so sharp he can shave hair on his arm and even then, even then he does not hurry.

There is another cup of coffee and another Bull Durham cigarette and still another cup of coffee and at last out into the cool fall morning air the knife in one hand and a piece of rag in the other.

87

The pig stands, watching, waiting, its head down and cocked sideways, waiting perhaps to be fed, to be doctored, to be scratched behind the ear, waiting for all the things pigs wait for but the one thing that is coming. Must come.

It is fast and takes years, all at the same time. Two men are needed. They both enter the pen, one with the knife hidden behind his leg. They push the pig into a corner with their legs, push him and hold him and then in one motion they reach down and turn him on his back and he knows, he knows and the scream starts but now there is speed, rolling speed in what is happening and when the pig is on his back one man kneels on him and spreads his front legs and the other kneels in front and slides the knife, curve side down, point first, up beneath the sternum on the pig and cuts the top artery on the heart, twists the knife a bit and the pig bleeds out.

That's how they say it.

The pig bleeds out.

But it is not clean and from the stick to the death is not short, not fast, and he screams, screams his life away and the men hold him on his back while it happens, while the pig bleeds out.

It is the way to kill a pig.

A pig must bleed, they say.

Cattle are different, chickens are different, but for this one animal, this one time it is the way to kill a pig and when it is done the men stand, while it is done the men stand away for

88

the last small part of the pig's life as it bleeds out on the ground, the last of the blood, they stand and always, always they look away. To take this one thing from the pig, the look says, to take the one thing the pig owns, his life, to take that away the look says, to take it for bacon . . .

Out across the pasture at the color on the leaves in the woods, at the sky lowering gray with autumn, they look at those things and they spit and they do not smile, they never smile and they are quiet.

The dog comes, and he smiles, and he works at the warm blood as it flows, licking at it, and the chickens come and peck at it and the other pig, which may die in a week, even he is excited by the blood, but the men do not smile.

With the killing of the pig, the first killing of the fall, there is work again and now it must be fast.

A huge pot of water has been brought to boil over a wood fire, first pine to get it going, then oak to keep it hot. The pig is pulled up on a pulley over the hot water, spread apart on two hooks that go through the tendons and lowered, lowered into the boiling water until he bends slightly and is covered then he is pulled out and scraped.

"Toothbrushes," somebody always says. "All your best tooth-brushes are made with pig bristles . . ."

The hair and bristles come out with the small circular scraper, even in the ears, every place to reach, and the dog waits and the cats wait.

When the hide is clean of the smallest hair the pot is dumped and taken away and the fire let to die and the pig is gutted. Hung upside down and zippered down with a knife, the same knife, and the guts coil and drop into a waiting tub.

Not to throw away. The heart is kept and the liver and the kidneys and the intestine kept and cleaned for sausage casing. Only the stomach is given to the dog and the bile sack, though an uncle swears he likes to sprinkle the bile on raw liver and eat it he never does, and the lungs and throat tubes. The dog eats them all, sharing involuntarily with the barn cats who are three and seem like thirty.

"Pigs have dotted lines," an uncle says. "For cutting . . ."

Which is not true except that there are places where one section joins another, not dotted lines but almost seams where a cut must be made.

First to split the pig. There is a clear joint in the back end, where the hams come together, and this can be cut apart and then the meat saw taken down the whole middle until every-thing is in half and then the halves are each cut in half just to the rear of the ribs and the hams are cut away and at last, when the hams are cut away and the back is cut in chops on the table in the kitchen and the liver is cooking with raw fried potatoes because liver cannot be kept, then it is possible to begin to forget about the pig screaming and bleeding. When all that is done and the meat is cooking and the smell of pepper takes the place of the smell of blood then it is not a pig any longer waiting to have its ears scratched but is meat.

Meat.

Everything must be done right. Hams and bacon and belly salted and smoked and cured. The smokehouse is down at the back of the yard, south of the house so the smoke will blow away. It is of wood and logs chinked with mud and a small piece of chimney to let the smoke out after it has gone up through the hams and bacons hanging on crosspieces.

All of hardwood. No pine because the resin will spoil the meat. No pine and no birch because it makes a taste, a birch taste, but oak and maple and ironwood, all in a cookpit connected to the smokehouse by a chimney buried underground.

It's impossible to not look.

They say you can't look, the old ones, because it will ruin the taste if you hurry it by looking but it is impossible not to peek into the smokehouse and see the hams hanging there, the salt and sugar cure crusted on them, hanging on the polished hardwood shafts next to the sausages and the slabs of bacon. The color makes the spit come, the smell makes the stomach rumble and knot, but it cannot be eaten until midwinter, the ham and bacon, until other meat is exhausted.

The killing doesn't stop with the pigs.

Hogs. When they are for slaughter in some way the name changes and they are called hogs.

The killing doesn't stop with the hogs but only starts. Next come chickens for canning and a beef when the weather is cold enough for storing meat.

Not winter cold, not yet, but there is a morning when the water in the stock tank by the barn has an inch of ice on top and has to be chopped with an axe and the old ones joke about not sticking your tongue on the pump handle or it will stick, which of course makes all the children dare each other to stick their tongues on the pump handle—comes that morning and it is time to kill a beef.

Not a cow then, not a calf fed to suck on fingers in warm milk in a bucket, not a milk cow to nestle the forehead into while listening to the drum of milk hitting the bucket nor a cow to touch and pet as it leaves the barn to head for spring or summer pasture, no. None of that now.

It is beef.

A steer. And here the kill is quick. The .22 rifle, the utility gun, the rusted .22 stuck on the deer antlers on the front porch that is used for skunks and weasels and hawks or owls taking chickens or foxes coming into the coop or to shoot cans from the tops of fence posts, that gun. That gun.

One shot.

Make a cross from each eye to the opposite ear. The small cross and just where the lines would meet that is where. One shot there and down, down so fast the beef seems pulled down, jerked down, hard down on its chest by the little .22 and then fast, so fast two men roll it on its side and cut across the throat to bleed it out for the few moments the heart still pumps after the shot and to catch the blood in a dishpan for blood sausage made in bread pans and baked in the oven at slow heat to be cut and refried with morning potatoes.

So much meat. Much of the beef will be canned but what isn't will be stored in the cool room of the granary where it will freeze, so much meat and still not enough.

Chickens are not just canned but will be killed through the year as they are needed for Sunday dinners. The meat and killing and more meat and more killing seem to fill the whole autumn and meat is eaten and liver and kidneys are eaten and heart is eaten until hair glistens and everybody is red and thick with meat but still, still it is not enough. Not enough meat for the year, for the winter.

There is one more kind of meat.

And one morning, early, before daylight, before anybody is up in the house, one morning early a new quiet comes, a soft quiet, and in the moonlight from the dormer window up in the upstairs of the house, in the attic of the house where there is no heat except what filters up through the stairwell, out from beneath the deep quilts and through the dormer window around the icy edges there is snow.

New snow.

First snow. First lovely new snow of fall, two inches, four inches, six inches of clean white covering all things, sitting on fence posts and on fence rails, making the granaries look like gingerbread houses in the moonlight with soft curves of white and gentle corners.

Always so clean, the first snow, so new and clean and fresh that the young have to be in it, *must* be in it, and before daylight they are outside, making snow angels and fighting and rolling and sitting on the grain shovel to slide down the bank next to the frozen stream in back of the barn.

An aunt, bundled in a man's coat, an older aunt comes out and sits on the porch with five-buckle overshoes dangling and she has a bowl with cream, fresh cream thick from last night's milking and separating, and she mixes fresh new snow with the cream and sprinkles coarse sugar on it and eats with a small spoon, her little finger held up delicately and a soft young smile on her mouth while her feet wave back and forth and she studies the marvel that was her yard.

It will mean work, this first fall snow, and more work, but when it first comes it is for children to play in and for an aunt to eat with cream and sugar and for the men and for the boys it means hunting.

Deer hunting.

Every fall when the first snow is there for tracking, the last meat of the year must be taken. Venison. They call it deer hunting, treat it like deer hunting and act like they are going to hunt, but it is not. It is taking wild meat because even with the two hogs and the chickens and the beef canned and stored

in the granary, even with all the killing that has taken place, it is not enough meat. Not for how they live, not for how they are working sixteen, eighteen hours a day with no letup, work that won't ever let up takes more than vegetables and cookies. It takes meat, and to kill your own meat for all of it, to keep killing hogs and beef and chickens, it becomes too expensive and so there are deer.

Another kind of meat.

"Used to shoot them off the corn like crows," the old ones say. "Used to come in by the hundreds and ruin the corn, same as bears, and we'd have to shoot them off and didn't keep nothing but the back legs for venison hams and the tenderloin for good gravy. Shot them like rabbits."

Now it is different.

Not hunting, but organized killing of meat. Again the families join, as they did with threshing and haying, the men from the families come together to hunt not with slick weapons and fancy clothes. The guns are all lever action .30-.30, Winchester or Marlin and old, some of them older than the men shooting them, with worn octagonal barrels and vernier peep sights screwed to the tang, so old they shot wolves, these guns, so old they might have shot at Indians. But cared for, oiled, kept in covered cases not like the .22 on the deer antlers on the porch but in a room in the house.

There will be venison or there will not be venison, there will be fat meals through the coming winter or there will not be so many fat meals and much of that, much of the reason for that comes down on the rifle and how well the man shoots the rifle, and they are cared for the way the threshing machine is cared for, the way the sickle bar or the Pittman arm on the haymower is cared for, another machine to get another job done.

There is of course the ritual.

Up before.

Up before any time anybody ever arose in the morning, up before all things, up while still asleep, and out into the barn to do chores in the cold morning with the ice crinkling under overshoes and the shoulders huddled in under the mackinaw, trying to hold in the bed warmth from the quilts, out into the barn to feed and clean and milk and separate before—up before.

Before the gathering.

There are plans. Nothing is left to chance. There are plans.

Men and boys arrive in trucks and old cars, radiators steaming, and they park next to the house and come in. The men sit at the table, drinking coffee and eating piles of cookies to supplement the breakfast they have eaten only minutes before and sucking sugar lumps in the light of the Coleman lantern because it is still dark, pitch dark, and the boys stand back in a circle and lean against the wall.

And there are plans.

Traced with fingers on the oilcloth tablecloth in the cookie crumbs there are these plans.

"We'll come through Halversons' first," they say, "because they'll be holed up in there in those tamarack swamps and not moving yet. We'll take them out of there and then we can take them over to Ellingsons'. Once they're moving they'll go to Ellingsons' and when we've done that we'll sweep that half section in back of Halversons'. That should do her."

When they say "we'll sweep," when the men say that "we'll take them out," they don't mean "we" they mean that the young will do the sweeping. The men post at clearings and with their rifles, post with jars full of coffee and lips full of fresh snuff and a sandwich in their pockets and their rifles and wait for the deer to run out past them.

The young, the boys sweep through the woods. Younger boys have nothing, no weapons, and carry sticks that they beat on trees and make whooping sounds and yell at each other to drive the deer.

Not deer, now, but venison the way the cow became beef and the pig became a hog.

The venison must be driven out of the woods to the waiting rifles where they will be dropped as sure as if they had been in a pen near the barn and the little .22 had been used to put a bullet where the line crosses from eye to ear.

That sure.

The younger boys have no weapons but the older boys carry old guns, single barrel shotguns loaded with slugs or nine pieces of buckshot or a .30-.30 with barrels so pitted and rusted they cannot shoot straight or break-open double barrel shotguns with damascus twist barrels that must shoot black powder loads older than some of the men who are waiting for the venison to come.

For the young it is possible to go a whole season and never see a live deer. For the boys who sweep the woods. The swamp grass is waist high, often covered with up to another foot of snow, and must be waded through, fought through mile after mile while yelling and beating against trees with sticks and perhaps carrying a long barreled old singleshot shotgun taller than the boy, the barrel catching on every twig, directions getting mixed and pushed until everything is soaked, snow is down inside clothes and all parts of deer hunting are hated and there is a deer.

First deer.

It comes from nowhere, can't possibly be there, standing not twenty thirty fifteen yards away, side on.

A buck.

It stands, perfectly still, and looks with small jets of steam coming out of its nostrils, its rack glistening in the cold air, looks at the boy, the young man, the child with his gun, looks and stands and the boy raises the old shotgun, his chest heaving, his hands and arms shaking, and holds on the deer, on the buck, holds and it is all there, first man, first love, first time first breath first first first.

First deer.

He fires.

Recoil slams him back, knocks him down into the snow and swamp grass but not before he sees the slug take the deer, not before he sees the punch in back of the shoulder and just high, just high but there, where he aimed or near it the punch and the hair that seems to jump out around where the slug went in not before that, not before he sees that.

Not before he sees that the deer doesn't move except to jerk a bit with the punch, doesn't move and turns to look at him, right at him, into his eyes, and then sinks, sinks to the ground as if going to sleep, taking a sleep with its antlers back on its shoulders nestled in the hair there, the tips laid back and the throat up, and another boy comes who had been driving beside, comes and says:

"Holy shit, you got one."

In a soft voice. Almost a prayer and the deer is dead, the eyes glazed with it, with the end, the deer is gone and all that is left is venison.

First deer.

First venison.

And of course buck fever comes and the boy shakes and cannot control the shaking and the two boys forget what needs to be done, forget to drop the guts and begin to drag the deer out of the swamp head first, pulling on the antlers, but still with all the added weight of the guts still in him.

A mile in swamp grass and waist-high snow, a mile and more dragging the dead buck and all the boy can see is the glazed eyes on the dead deer and think how the buck looked at him right after the shot, the way the buck looked into him, right into his eyes.

"He looked at me," he says, dragging at the deer with the second boy. "He looked at me."

"Of course he did—hell, you shot him. Who else would he look at?"

First deer and the look never goes and the boy swears he will never kill again, never kill another deer and thinks that each day but it grows weaker all the time, the memory, and the next year he will be there again, deer hunting.

When all the woods have been driven and all the hunting is done the deer are divided equally among the families. Sixteen, seventeen twenty deer, mostly bucks but some does, and each family gets three or four deer and still, still it is not enough meat for all the year.

The deer are skinned and halved and the halves stored in the granary where they will remain frozen for the winter next to the beef, pieces cut off them for stew or meat gravy to cover potatoes, strips to fry in butter, chunks to mix with pork for hot beans on impossibly cold winter days.

And when deer hunting is done and the days do not grow

warm any longer but just become light and then dark again and the darkness seems longer than the light, when the new snow isn't new and the aunt no longer comes to sit on the porch and eat snow with cream and sugar, when the quilts in the attic dormer room are so warm they cannot be removed and feet put on cold floors, when all the mice in the world seem to try to move into the house until a dozen traps are filled each night with them, jumping and snapping, and the ice on the pond is so thick it cannot be chopped through then . . .

Then it has come.

Winter.

WINTER

WINTER IS A TIME FOR THE FARM TO REST, THEY SAY, FOR THE soil to lie beneath the snow and ice and get ready for the next year, a time to prepare, but that is not so, not so because in winter it all must go on, the work must go on except that now it is harder to be outside where all the work waits, outside in the cold and snow. There are things the old ones say when they feel winter has come.

"So cold you could spit and it bounces."

"So cold you could take a piss and lean on it . . ."

It is so cold and the snow is so deep and the ice is so thick and the trees so brittle and the walls so thin and the boots so worn that every winter, every winter is worse than the one before even if it isn't, always it is.

Winter stories are like thresher stories and corn chopper stories.

"He wasn't gone two, three hours and they went looking for him and found him sitting by the side of the straw pile frozen solid, dead. And he was only three years old."

"The wind was so bad it blew snow under your eyelids, was it back in nineteen and ten or nineteen and eleven? So bad you couldn't see your hand and he left to go to the barn and never got there, never got there. They found him just off to the side forty feet. Walked forty feet past the barn, he did, missed it by just forty feet and they found him frozen stiff dead. They said he looked like he was praying, on his knees looking up with the snow in his eyes not melted. Said he was praying."

Winter grips, they say.

Spring opens, summer lets, fall gathers, and winter grips.

First there is wood. Firewood must be taken in and stored and this cannot be done until there is enough solid snow for the bobsled.

Two sleds with oak runners and steel shoes, two sleds one in front of the other hooked together with X-chains on slick steel shoes and crosspieces with poles sticking up on either side to hold the wood in and the teams know, the horses know the difference and like to pull the bobsled.

Out of the barn dressed in the steam of their breath and off their backs, steam around them, they are brought harnessed from the barn and hooked back into the bobsled, the oak tongue between them, and they prance.

"Look at Bob, he's like a colt," an uncle says. "Like a goddamn colt, look at him."

Prancing, great feet clopping down into the ice, they are hooked by trace-and-chain to the bobsled and the ride into the woods is a great flaming screaming run through white-coated trees and fallen timbers.

It takes half a mile of pulling on the reins to slow them and then they are still prancy and dancy and full of themselves and have to be tied off hard to a tree to hold them while firewood is loaded.

Later there will be logging, serious work, but now it is only for firewood. Only dead wood is taken, standing dead popples that hardly need to be sawed. Many can be pushed over with the hand and laid on the bunk of the bobsled by hand and the load is not heavy even when it is piled high in the bunks. So high it cannot be seen over, so high it takes a climb to get up on top and cluck the team into motion to head back to the yard.

And again.

There is never enough meat and there is never enough firewood. Each time the bobsled is filled and emptied the pile fills and grows and it is still not enough.

"Cut and stacked the woodpile should be the same size as the house," they say, the old ones. "And that doesn't count the kitchen stove."

Dry wood burns hot and burns fast and popple burns almost

as fast as dry pine but there isn't enough oak for firewood, some but not enough, and so popple must be used and so the pile grows with each load until it seems not as big as the house but larger, so high of all long logs that it seems impossible to cut it all.

Every stick.

When it is full, when it is higher than the snow-covered straw pile it must be cut and stacked and the larger pieces split so they will stay dry in the middle and the cutting is the last use of the tractor for the year.

It has been drained because the water will freeze and crack the block, so the radiator and block are filled with warm water to take the chill from the steel and the tractor is started one more time, the flywheel cranked until it kicks and bucks and she's going, going. The belt, the same belt that was used to drive the threshing machine is used to drive a three-foot file-sharpened saw blade on a steel frame, drive it so that it whirrs and two men position themselves, stand to the blade.

One on one side of the screaming cutting edge, one on the other. A log is picked up by one man, fed across the blade where the other man grabs the end, large end first, and the two men pull the log into the blade.

There is a scream, almost a pig-death scream, and the log is snipped off and the man holding the cut end throws it off into the snow while the man holding the log pushes it forward where the end can be grabbed again and pushed against the saw blade with another harsh scream and another piece of firewood flies through the air to land in the snow where there will be a pile of wood as large as the house or larger.

One stick at a time.

"Firewood warms you five times," the old ones say. "When you bring it in from the woods, when you cut it, when you split it, when you carry it into the house, and when you burn it. Five times."

The rhythm of the cutting, the pushing the log forward, grabbing the end, pushing it against the blade, throwing it, pushing it forward, grabbing it, against the blade, throwing it—the mindless rhythm repeated thousands of times makes for boredom and the boredom makes for mistakes.

Wood cutting stories are like corn chopping stories and blizzard stories.

"It was fast, so fast you couldn't see it. He took off four fingers right where he was holding the log, pushed it and took them off clean and threw the log into the pile and reached for the next log before he knew they were gone. The fingers fell off to the side and the dog got one of them and went away with it. He never did like that dog again, old Oscar. Hated that dog the rest of his life."

The firewood is the first true act of winter and the pile of wood is concern for everybody. At some time during the cutting an aunt will come out and view the pile critically, study it from several sides and say softly:

"Seems a bit thin."

Even though all the long logs aren't cut up yet, even though the stack isn't finished and the cutting and stacking have gone on for six lifetimes, she must be right, must always be right because each year it is the same, each year she views the pile and shakes her head and says gently, "Seems a bit thin," and more wood is brought in and cut and added to the pile and it is never too much. Never.

Almost to a stick each year the wood is burned, all the wood, and when she comes out to see the pile and says that, says it's too thin, an uncle smiles at a brother and at a boy and shakes his head and says: "More wood for the house—we'll need more."

Snow comes.

More snow until the straw pile and the silage pit are covered with two, three feet of new snow and there is a drift that comes up to the edge of the barn roof where it slants down so a slide can be made by pouring warm water down the roof and onto the drift. By aiming carefully, banking the snow, the young working harder at this than they ever would at gathering wood or threshing or haying, by working and banking and making the curves just so, it is possible to sit in a grain shovel with the legs raised and approach terminal velocity by the time the bottom is reached. Down off the roof, onto the drift, curve to the left and down the back hill of the farmyard and out onto the stock pond at twenty, thirty, forty, fifty miles an hour so

fast everything blurs, so fast breath leaves the lungs, so fast if a turn is missed snow is jam-packed into every opening in clothing and body.

Grease the shovel.

Pour more water on the slide, down through the drift. More still, until it is pure ice all the way.

Faster still. Faster and faster slamming around the corners sitting in the grain shovel until finally someone breaks an arm leg wrist ankle nose, cuts a forehead or cheek and runs to the house and the sliding is stopped.

Until two days, three days, a week have passed and another slide is made or snow forts appear.

Snow forts where there is all the ammunition in the world, snow bullets, snow cannon, snow wars that end always in disaster, end always in blood because snowballs are never enough and somebody wraps a piece of ice with snow and somebody else gets hit in the nose, always the nose and there is blood.

Early winter games. When the snow is still wet enough to stick. Great forts, great wars that turn the barnyard into a battleground, the granary into a castle, games through November and into December until a day comes, the day, and an uncle walks into the woods near the house and comes out with a tree to nail boards to the bottom and set it up in the sitting room in the corner opposite the stove.

Christmas.

A hidden time that comes suddenly, tree in the sitting room decorated with strips of tin cut from cans for tinsel and popcorn and scraps of colored yarn and cloth and packages wrapped in paper saved from last year and the year before and the year before, saved for each Christmas the paper to wrap presents, saved and folded and kept up in the bedroom closet for the presents.

A pocketknife. A pair of knitted mittens or a pair of knitted wool socks with a red band around the top. Carved toys of soft wood that looks like polished honey shaped in a team of horses with a bobsled. A handmade pair of skis.

A scarf with color to match eyes. A small box of stationery bought with hidden parts of the small money from the eggs for Christmas, for presents.

Two Christmases.

One for the presents and the food. A table filled, the kitchen filled with smell and taste, use the ham from the pig saved through Thanksgiving, a saved ham to eat until only the bone is left and then to strip the taste from the bone in soup to cook on the back of the stove for days.

Two Christmases.

One for the food and the presents and coming down the stairwell in the morning to see what can have happened in the night. That Christmas. One for the tree and the rustle of paper and the pure mystery of not knowing, never really knowing what will be in the rustling paper.

112

But two Christmases.

The one for the tree and the presents and the food and the morning and the paper and the other one for God.

For God.

A Christmas to sit the night before while an uncle reads from the Bible through dollar glasses bought from a mail-order house, his finger moving like a blunt stick with the words as he reads the story of Christmas. A Christmas to think of Herod and Bethlehem and Mary and the baby Jesus and to look out the window at the stars and wonder if they are the same now over the farm as they were then over the shepherds and their flocks and to think of God and his Son and how that can be, how all that can be and to stay awake, hold awakeness until midnight to troop to the barn bundled in coats over pajamas to see if the animals really do talk at midnight on Christmas Eve.

Two Christmases. One for the farm and the presents and the food but the other one for God, there on that one day, the bright day with sun on snow and cold coming through the windows to hit the heat from the stove in early winter, a day for God and then, suddenly the paper is all wrapped and put away in the closet for next year and a day has come when early winter is gone.

Too soon gone and high winter sets in.

Cold.

Cold now that doesn't stop with the short daylight but work

113

goes on. When early winter play is done and the woodpile is at last large enough true winter work sets in.

Woodcutting.

Not firewood now but pulpwood to sell for the paper mills. Cordwood. Stickwood. Moneywood.

In all the summer, in all the harvest, in all the work on the farm and for the farm there is no money. No work for money, no thing for money, no money. Cream and eggs are for the house, to be sold for the house, and it is small money, tiny money for the house and perhaps some corner of it set aside for Christmas, for candy at Christmas or decorations.

Small money.

And the potato-picking money is for the young, for clothes and maybe a little more, but it is gone as well, spent really in dreams before it is earned.

But money is needed.

For the farm, there is money needed.

A Pittman arm can be made, but not the wheel it turns, not the sickle bar it pushes. Mower teeth wear out, can be sharpened for a while but will each year wear and be gone and new ones must be purchased. Some machinery is always breaking down, snapping or twisting or warping or gouging or bending and new parts must be sent for, must be bought.

With money.

Always there is money needed. And never is there enough of it. Never enough money.

But the paper mills will buy wood, buy cordwood if it is stacked by the railroad tracks, cut in eight-foot lengths, measured and cut and stacked neatly along the tracks, they'll buy the wood.

For money.

So when the firewood is all in and early winter is past and the machinery is laid down and in sheds the time for winter work comes, the time for woodcutting, pulp cutting.

It is where the men make pride—that is what the old ones say. You farm to live, work to live, but pride comes with an axe.

Two-bladed axe. Name it, they say—it's a Diamond double bladed. Diamond holds the best edge, cuts the cleanest. "See now, see Gustaf—when he was young he was a bull. He could cut off an eight-inch tree in two cuts, so clean the tree seemed to jump off the stump."

How sharp is his axe, how clean the cut, how low the stump. Cut it high and you lose length on the thick end, lose length and lose money.

Cut her low, cut her even with the ground, oh yes, cut her smooth and clean and pop the limbs off with forward and backward swings as fast as a man can walk the length of the downed tree.

And where does it fall?

On big trees, balsams and pine, the axe cuts an aiming notch, low and perfectly cut, and the two man bucksaw is used to cut the tree off and it drops, always drops just so, just there, just there and clean and down.

And the horses wait.

While the men stoop low and the bucksaw hisses and the trees drop, one and another the horses wait with the bobsled, wait in the steam of their breath, wait to pull.

But not yet.

Was a day, was a day the old ones say not so long back when there weren't all the railroads and the horses only pulled logs in great loads to the nearest river and the logs would be floated down to the mill in the spring.

But not now.

Now the railroads are the river and sometimes the horses have to pull the load two, three, four miles from where they cut; the sled jamming them forward when it goes downhill, slams the collars into their necks when they go uphill.

So the horses wait. They know and they wait.

Trees are dropped and limbs cleaned off and two men use the bucksaw to cut the wood into eight-foot pieces to load on the sled in the bunks, eight foot and eight foot up in sections to the tops to leave piled by the limbs, brush on top of the snow for the rabbits, the snowshoe rabbits to use for shelter from the cold that comes now.

High winter cold.

Wood is hauled to the railroad and the sled comes back at

dark, empty, the horses running to get to the warm barn and the oats there and the hay.

Chores are done, and there is sleep, soft sleep from the cows with their breathing filling the barn with heat and the smooth sound of their chewing, as they bring up their cuds, mixes with the low rumble of the barn cats purring and the sigh of the horses' stomachs as they digest the oats and get ready for the next day in the woods.

Barnsleep.

Down and soft and safe barnsleep.

The barn is cleaned and it is early yet but pitch dark when the men come in, done for the day except for work that can be done in the house with the Coleman lantern hissing overhead in the flat white light that fuses with the orange from the mica window on the front of the stove.

The winter is still on faces, the cold and wind and ice and snow lasts on faces red and burnt and hot after food, after the canned meat and gravy and potatoes, and still it is not late, not that late, not summer late, and so to the sitting room.

Never used in summer nor in spring nor in fall, never used, dusted and cleaned but never used because there is never time until winter.

Then the stove is there and the Coleman light is turned off and two kerosene lamps are lighted on end tables where they sit on doilies crocheted the winter before and the winter before

117

and the winter before, doilies pressed in sugar water to keep them stiff and white to catch the yellow light of the lamps and the glow from the stove and everybody sits.

In the old chair there is a grandmother out in the floor with a quilting frame working to turn rags into beauty, her hands never still, never still even when she smiles and laughs or cries at the stories.

An uncle sits near the stove on a wooden chair brought from the kitchen. Across his lap is a bucksaw sitting on a rag and he has a small three-cornered file that he uses to sharpen the teeth on the saw, not set but to sharpen, and when the saw is done there is another saw and when that is done he uses a round stone to hone axes, which are head down in an old bucket next to him, hone them until they will cut hair off his arm like a razor with a soft coat of lard to them when they are sharp, and to the saws to make them cut and slip better and keep them from rusting and when they are at last finished he will fill his lip with snoose and bring the spit can close to his ankle by the chair and lean back and tell the stories.

An aunt sits on one end of the old horsehair sofa that once was soft but is getting hard, sewing a patch on overalls, and on the other end there is a daughter who is not a child any longer and so does not sit on the floor but on the sofa with her mother and crochets, seeking beauty in the yarn that comes together, sits with her mother and near her grandmother and all of it is there, all the beauty in the yarn and quilt and the three women sitting together is there waiting, waiting for the stories.

And on the floor are the children. Fighting to stay awake, bellies full as pups would be full, round and tight and full with fat cheeks red and always a cowlick, sitting with eyes that bounce open and close while the heat from the stove works to put them to sleep, they wait for the stories.

An uncle spits in the can again and the axes are sharp and the saws are sharp and greased and he takes a sip of coffee from the large pot always on the back of the stove, a cup first thing in the morning and last thing at night, a cup of eggshell coffee he sips and he clears his throat and he starts:

"Was a time when Clarence Engerson was just here from the old country, just here and he wanted to buy a team of horses and had no money. Damn, that was a hard time then. No money. So he had to work them off and it was so that he worked to pay for the team so hard that he used the days up and had to farm his own place in the dark. Ha! Used to call him the night farmer, we did—night farmer Clarence. But damn, he made good potatoes . . ."

Stories of love and death and cold and heat and ice and flame, stories sad and stories happy and stories of laughter and tears and places soft and hard, of crops never made and crops to fill granaries, stories of great men and beautiful women and souls and devils and gods, stories of lost dreams and found joys and aches and torture and great rolling hills and storms

119

and things quick and hot and slow and dull, stories of graves and horses, pigs and kings, war and the times between wars, stories of children's cheeks and the soft hair at a woman's temple when it is moist, stories of rage and spirit and shit and blood and bodies on fences and hay so sweet you could eat the grass, oh God yes, stories of all things there in the winter by the stove in the sitting room never used in summer or fall or spring, stories to quicken, to make the hair go up on the back of the neck and stop the breath and bring life.

Stories that are everything, all of everything there is, the stories.

Winterstories.

Each night in the cold deep winter, each night the stories while the saws are sharpened and the axes are honed, stories each night until eyes close and weave the stories into a dream world as the yarn becomes beauty when it is crocheted, until sleep must come and the young walk up the stairwell to the dormer attic rooms where there is no heat and they bundle into the quilts to sleep looking out ice-rimmed windows at a blue-white moon on the brittle cold of high winter snow, sleep in the warm quilts as the land sleeps as all things sleep after the stories, waiting for winter to end.

Waiting.